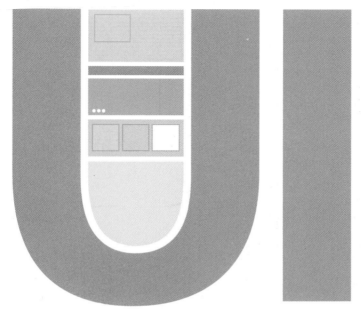

DESIGN
with Adobe® Illustrator®

Rick Moore

ADOBE
PRESS

Adobe

UI Design with Adobe® Illustrator®
Rick Moore

Adobe Press books are published by:

Peachpit
1249 Eighth Street
Berkeley, CA 94710
510/524-2178
800/283-9444

Peachpit is a division of Pearson Education.
For the latest on Adobe Press books, go to
www.adobepress.com.
To report errors, please send a note to errata@peachpit.com.
Copyright © 2013 by Rick Moore

Adobe Press Editor: Victor Gavenda
Project Editor: Nancy Peterson
Development Editor: Stephen Nathans-Kelly
Technical Editor: Tom Johnson
Copyeditor: Darren Meiss
Production Editor and Compositor: Danielle Foster
Indexer: Joy Dean Lee
Cover design: Aren Howell Straiger
Interior design: Mimi Heft

ISBN 13: 978-0-321-83385-3
ISBN 10:   0-321-83385-6

987654321

Printed and bound in the United States of America

For Shelley, Cali, and Carice; my favorite girls in the whole world.

Acknowledgments

Writing a technical book is crazy hard, and this adventure would not have been possible without the help of so many people. First, thanks to my wife, Shelley, for her encouragement, support, understanding, and love as I undertook this wild endeavor. I could never have done this without you. Thanks to my daughters, Cali and Carice, for being patient while Dad was holed up in his office banging away at a keyboard for six months. Let's go play now!

Huge thanks go to Denise Jacobs for tons of helpful advice and for putting me in touch with the right people to make this a reality. I never could have gotten it started without your help. Thanks to Victor Gavenda who got the ball rolling. Thanks to my superstar editor, Nancy Peterson, and her team, Stephen Nathans-Kelly and Darren Meiss, for all the time and effort spent bringing my words to life and making me sound like I know what the heck I'm talking about. Thanks to my tech editor, Tom Johnson, for methodically checking and questioning my instructions so that they make sense to you, the reader. Finally, thanks to Mimi Heft, Danielle Foster, and all the other production people working behind the scenes to make this book look great.

Thanks to all of my coworkers, friends, and professionals who provided ideas, feedback, and support before, during, and after the process: Colt Pini, Nic Johnson, Kaleb Tracy, Juna Duncan, Albert Candari, Jared Lewandowski, Ty Hatch, Michelle Barber, Clifton Labrum, David Lindes, Cameron Moll, and Khoi Vinh.

Thanks to my mentors who helped me immensely as I started my journey into the world of user experience: Gilbert Lee, John Dilworth, Rob Thomas, Todd Ericksen, and the entire NorthTemple team. You guys rock. I miss the old days.

Contents

Introduction

UI Design with Adobe Illustrator

I realize right off the bat that I am going to date myself here. I began my career as a graphic designer when the web was still in its infancy. I learned paste-up techniques and created marker comps before I ever knew that same stuff could be done faster on a computer. Once I got out of school, it became apparent very quickly that those skills, while useful, were pretty much obsolete. To get with the times, I bought myself the only computer I could afford at the time, a shiny new Wintel PC, added a copy of CorelDraw, and started down the path of digital graphic design. Little did I know that many years later my print skills would rarely be put into use. Right around that same time, I got an Earthlink account and started a web page on Geocities as a playground for learning HTML, which at the time was nothing more than a curiosity.

A Web Start

I bought my first Mac in 1998, then designed and built my first client website that same year (**I.A**). I used Photoshop to mock up the pages and slice up the graphics for a (gasp) table-based layout. Dreamweaver was utilized to write the markup. I remember the joy I experienced watching that first site come to life, as crude and unrefined as it was compared to what is possible today. In the many years since that first site, I have tried to hone my workflow to be the most efficient it could be, but have always struggled in finding a way that felt as fast as it was creative.

In recent years, my career has shifted into the field of interaction design and user interface design. All the skills I learned as a graphic and web designer were taken to a whole new level while creating UIs for web applications and mobile devices. Like many in my profession, I used Photoshop daily to complete my design tasks. I loved the program for its ability to create pixel-perfect mockups. The thing

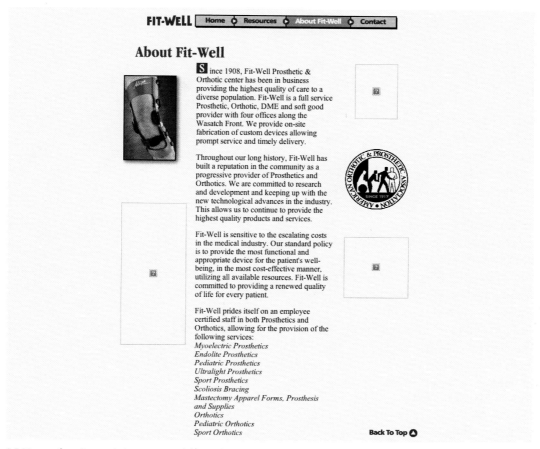

About Fit-Well

Since 1908, Fit-Well Prosthetic & Orthotic center has been in business providing the highest quality of care to a diverse population. Fit-Well is a full service Prosthetic, Orthotic, DME and soft good provider with four offices along the Wasatch Front. We provide on-site fabrication of custom devices allowing prompt service and timely delivery.

Throughout our long history, Fit-Well has built a reputation in the community as a progressive provider of Prosthetics and Orthotics. We are committed to research and development and keeping up with the new technological advances in the industry. This allows us to continue to provide the highest quality products and services.

Fit-Well is sensitive to the escalating costs in the medical industry. Our standard policy is to provide the most functional and appropriate device for the patient's well-being, in the most cost-effective manner, utilizing all available resources. Fit-Well is committed to providing a renewed quality of life for every patient.

Fit-Well prides itself on an employee certified staff in both Prosthetics and Orthotics, allowing for the provision of the following services:
Myoelectric Prosthetics
Endolite Prosthetics
Pediatric Prosthetics
Ultralight Prosthetics
Sport Prosthetics
Scoliosis Bracing
Mastectomy Apparel Forms, Prosthesis and Supplies
Orthotics
Pediatric Orthotics
Sport Orthotics

Back To Top ◯

I.A My very first client website courtesy of the Wayback Machine (www.archive.org/web/web.php). There used to be images there…really.

I liked least about it was its lack of flexibility in performing said task. I did have another tool in my design quiver that I used often, but mostly as a supplement to Photoshop. That application was Adobe Illustrator, which I loved for its speed and its vector-drawing chops. I tried through several versions to use it for mocking up web pages and application UIs, only to end up getting no further than wireframes and ultimately reverting back to Photoshop to finish the job.

Then something marvelous happened. In early 2010, Adobe released Illustrator CS5 with some pretty spiffy pixel-related features. Despite the problems I'd had previously and after some hesitation in upgrading, I decided to give it a go. And wouldn't you know it, the stars aligned and I was able to move my workflow to this tool without looking back. With the latest version, CS6, I have been able to become even faster and more efficient without ever hampering my creativity.

Who Needs This Book?

You might be a seasoned veteran and a Photoshop ninja, a budding designer fresh out of school, or someone with a good eye that needs help realizing their artistic vision. Whatever your background, this book aims to show you how to produce high-fidelity mockups in an extremely fast and efficient way. Although it covers some drawing techniques and tips for UI element creation, this is not a book that goes into great depth on how to create illustrative design. It's more focused on how to fit the pieces of your design together into a cohesive structure in order to craft the experience. Readers of any experience level will be able to find useful information.

> **NOTE** Notes are used throughout the book to alert you to important things to look for as you use an Illustrator tool or feature.

> **TIP** Tips provide you with additional information or techniques.

Today's websites and applications are so much different than they were when I started in the industry. For the web, HTML5 and CSS3 reduce the need for tons of graphics, and responsive design allows for those sites to adapt to the context of the device being used for browsing. I am firmly in the camp that in order to be a great designer, you need to know how to code what you design. It's important to understand how to design for the screen—no matter the size—and understanding the code helps you do just that. It's nothing like designing for the printed page. That being said, I don't follow the crowd that believes design should happen solely in a browser. For me, it happens more quickly on paper first and then in Illustrator. The techniques I cover in this book have made me faster at trying different ideas for a design before I mark them up or send them to development.

Sidebars

Look in the sidebars to find information that more thoroughly explains a tool or feature, as well as the explanation of more advanced concepts.

I.B Photoshop and Illustrator look and feel very similar. That helps a lot when it comes to learning a new tool.

An Air of Familiarity

If you have experience with Photoshop or InDesign, many of the concepts in Illustrator will seem very familiar. That's by design. Most of the apps in the Adobe Creative Suite share user interface conventions so they'll play well with each other (**I.B**), which makes the Illustrator learning curve much shorter. If you have never used any Adobe apps, all is not lost. You'll find the learning curve, while somewhat steep, fun to tackle and relatively easy to master. Like anything else, it's all about practice and patience. Once you get used to Illustrator, you'll have a hard time wondering why you never used it for web or app design before.

By the way, I am a keyboard-shortcut junkie. As they say, you learn by repetition, so I will repeat keyboard shortcuts throughout the book so that they will be easy to learn and remember. I really dislike choosing commands from menus. If you get nothing else from this book than a head full of keystrokes, you will have gotten your money's worth. That being said, I'll be sure to provide a couple different ways to do something and let you decide which works best for you. (Hopefully it's the shortcut route. Hint hint.)

Let's Get Started!

As a designer, I've used Illustrator for creating illustrations and designing logos for the majority of my career. Coming from using other applications for web design, though, is where I had to "unlearn" many of the habits I developed during those years. If you have never used Illustrator before, you may have an easier time getting settled in. As you open the program for the first time, you may be a little uneasy. The interface is fairly utilitarian and can be daunting at first. You may be looking at the tools, panels, and a big blank screen thinking, "Where do I even start?"

All of this power helps create a flexible workflow that works for you, rather than forces you to conform to the app. Illustrator is fairly customizable, so you can arrange panels, tools, and menus to suit your style and flow. Because of its object-based nature, it's easy to change your mind or experiment without fear.

I learn by doing, so this book teaches you how to use the tools in the creation of one screen of a UI mockup. Be sure to save your work as you go through the process. However, if you forget, you can download each stage of the mockup, as well as other helpful examples, by going to www.peachpit.com/UIwithAI. So, sit back, grab something refreshing to sip, and let creativity flow as you discover how to use Illustrator to realize your creative vision.

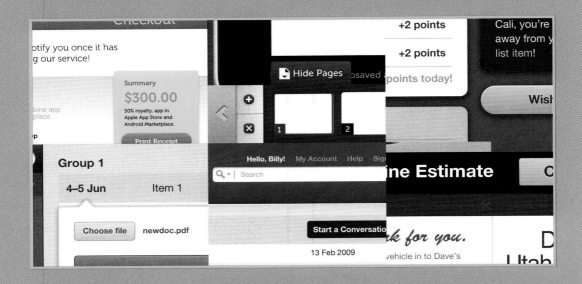

UI DESIGN WITH ADOBE ILLUSTRATOR: AN OVERVIEW

Chapter Overview

There are a lot of options on the market today for creating UI mockups and prototypes. They come with varying degrees of difficulty and a staggering range of features. One might say it's as hard to choose a mockup tool as it is to pick a computer platform.

Throughout my career, I have used several of these tools and have come to rely on Adobe Illustrator for my day-to-day work. It's loaded with features for professional UI design and is relatively easy to use. In this first chapter, you'll get a brief overview of some of the features that make Illustrator the perfect tool for creating high-fidelity mockups for your sites and apps:

- Vector-based drawing environment for flexibility
- Excellent color and typography tools
- Tools to help achieve design consistency
- Pixel-precise layouts

Let's dig in!

It's All About the Vector

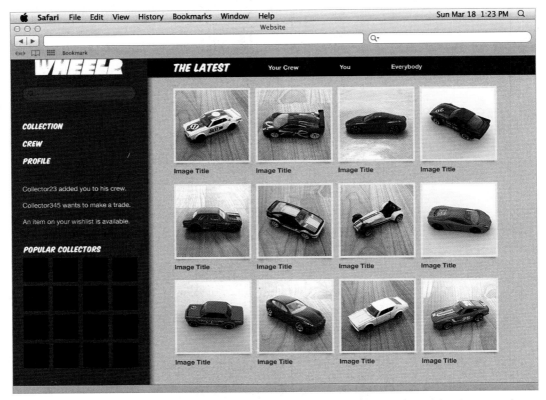

1.1 A typical application screen mockup has a much smaller file size in Illustrator. This entire design is less than a megabyte, even with photos.

Adobe Illustrator is a vector-based application. That means it uses mathematical expressions to draw points, lines, curves, and shapes on the screen to create graphics. In this way, Illustrator differs from a raster-based application like Photoshop that draws these same graphics with individual pixels. Vectors are inherently faster because computer processors can execute math instructions a lot faster than they can draw pixels.

The benefits for Illustrator users are many. To start, Illustrator just feels fast. Complex documents don't bog down your system and keep you from getting work done. Whether you're creating highly detailed UI mockups or simple wireframes, Illustrator chugs along without skipping a beat. Second, files don't consume as much storage space, allowing you to store more documents on your drive.

For example, the Illustrator file for a typical application screen mockup (**1.1**) weighs in at

883 KB. The same design saved as a layered Photoshop document is a hefty 4.4 MB. Add multiple screens or states into the Photoshop file and the size begins to increase exponentially. That may seem like a small file in comparison to high-resolution photos, but when you start to generate a lot of project files, it adds up quickly.

Third, vector graphics are scalable. For example, a design element created in Illustrator using vector shapes can be resized larger or smaller without affecting the quality of the graphic. Edges are always crisp, because all the computer has to do is redo the math to accommodate whatever change in size you made (**1.2** and **1.3**). It allows you to be more creative and spontaneous, because it frees you from having to think about the technical aspect of what you're creating. Let fear of client changes be a thing of the past.

Finally, Illustrator is very stable; I rarely experience crashes that steal away half a day's work like I did with my old Photoshop workflow. Notice that I didn't say *never*. Like any other software application on a computer bogged down with lots of activity, Illustrator is susceptible to scream-inducing crashes. You should really get in the habit of saving early and often. I've learned by sad experience that time still sometimes gets the better of me. I'll go an hour before saving my progress—that seems to be when crashes happen most. Murphy's Law, I guess.

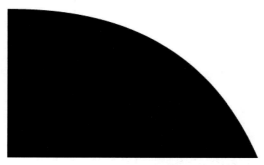

1.2 Vectors produce smooth edges that stay smooth when resized (shown here at 300% zoom).

1.3 Raster images pixelate when resized (shown here at 300% zoom).

Typography + Color = Power

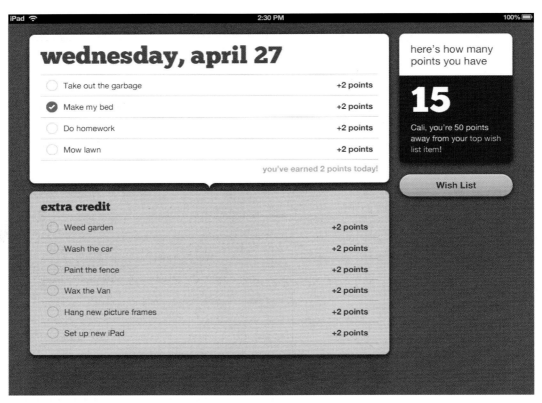

1.4 This screen design uses color and typography to create a visual hierarchy.

Typography and color theory are important principles of design. Adhering to or ignoring these principles can make or break the message or feeling you're trying to convey to your users. Illustrator's type and color tools help you to get that user-experience vision out of your head and onto the screen.

Typography for UI Design

If the content of your app delivers the experience you're trying to create, then good typography reinforces the voice of that experience. To help to achieve this synergy, Illustrator is stocked with professional-level typography tools (**1.5**). Truth be told, it's been one of Illustrator's strengths for a long time, but was made even better for UI design with the recent addition of anti-aliasing options.

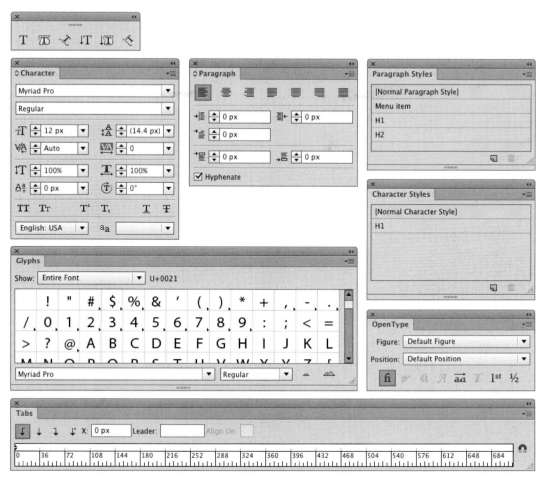

1.5 A bevy of typography tools gives users the power to create professional results.

Anti-aliasing adjusts how type looks on the screen by slightly blurring curved edges of letters to make them look as smooth as possible (**1.6**). Starting with Illustrator CS5, Adobe added additional anti-aliasing options from Photoshop. These new options allow you to more accurately simulate how type will render on your target devices. It's not 100% perfect, but it gets the job done.

No anti-aliasing

Anti-aliasing

1.6 Anti-aliasing smoothes the curved edges of a typeface to help it look better onscreen.

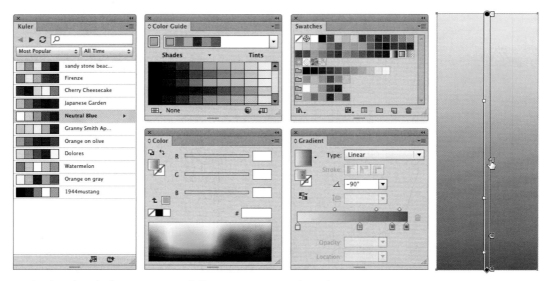

1.7 Get the right color for your project with Illustrator's extensive color tools.

Illustrator's flexible typesetting and extensive formatting tools give you tremendous agility when setting type. Character and Paragraph styles make formatting loads of text quick and easy. The Glyphs panel gives you access to any character in a typeface—no more hunting around the keyboard trying to find alternate characters, ornaments, or symbols. You can also wrap text around graphics in order to simulate browser floats in your design.

Powerful Tools for Color

Choosing the right color is fundamental to establishing a visual hierarchy and evoking emotion. Often, color speaks to your users in ways that content can't. Whether your design vision calls for a simple two-color palette or a complex system of color, Illustrator provides the tools you need to realize your vision.

Illustrator's color tools help you create the perfect color schemes and color any object with ease (**1.7**). There are several ways to apply color to your designs, allowing for maximum flexibility in your workflow. You can choose to use the default color swatches or go and make your own by mixing colors from one of several color models. Creating custom gradients is a cinch, and you can create and interact with them in a panel or directly on the object.

If, like me, you're one of the many designers who sometimes struggle with choosing the right colors, Illustrator can help you immensely with color harmony tools that take the guesswork out of color theory. With the Color Guide panel, you'll be able to build palettes using any of the standard color harmony rules and then vary your swatches based on included swatch libraries. You can even use Adobe's fantastic color inspiration tool, Kuler, right inside Illustrator.

Design for Consistency

One of the most time-consuming things to deal with in UI design is making sure that your design is consistent. Consistency is an extremely important attribute of great design. However, once you start working with multiple screens across several documents, keeping things consistent can become quite a chore. Illustrator addresses this need with several tools to help make the job easier.

For type, Illustrator's Paragraph and Character styles enable you to format text with a click (**1.8**). Gone are the days of trying to remember what font size you used on a headline, or what the leading value was for a standard bloc of body copy. Save these values in a style that can be used over and over again, just like you would with a word processor or page-layout app. You can also load them from one document into another so that you can maintain consistent typography as you begin to work with multiple documents.

You'll find it easy to design complete color schemes and combine the swatches together into portable swatch groups (**1.9**). These groups can be named and loaded into documents whenever you need them. This keeps you from having colors deviate between documents, creating inconsistencies that are a pain to fix.

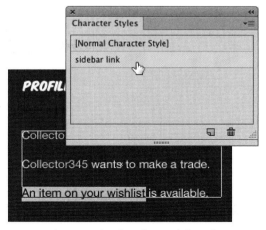

1.8 Using Character styles allows for one-click text formatting

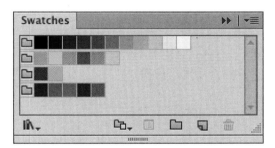

1.9 You can save color swatches in groups to create different color schemes.

Illustrator keeps track of how objects look with the Appearance panel. An *appearance* is a group of attributes that include an object's fill, stroke, transparency, and effects. You can style objects with ease using the Appearance panel and then save the appearance attributes as a graphic style. This graphic style can then be applied to other objects with one click (**1.10**). This automates the repetition of styling across similar elements, reducing time and effort to achieve consistency.

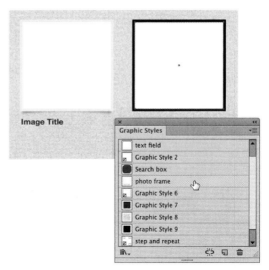

1.10 Complex designs saved as a graphic style can be applied to other objects in one click.

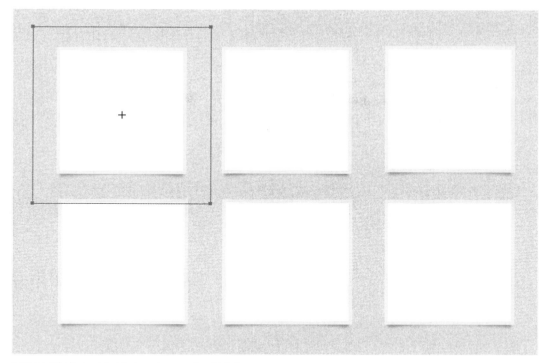

1.11 A symbol is an object that can be reused multiple times.

Design elements can be repeated easily using symbols. A *symbol* is an object that can be reused multiple times (**1.11**). In a document, a symbol can have multiple instances that are based on the original symbol. Where this helps with consistency is that if the original object changes, all the instances are automatically updated to reflect the changes. Conversely, symbols can be resized without affecting the original.

Another feature that enables consistency is the ability to create a template. You'll be able to save document settings, color schemes, graphic styles, character and paragraph styles, and symbols into the template and save it as a separate file. You can then use this template to create a new document that contains everything you need to get started.

Finally, you can "componentize" certain design elements by saving them as separate files and then importing them into a document. This feature is awesome if you work regularly with an interface design that spans multiple documents. When you import a file, it creates a link to the original. Any changes you make to the original file automatically updates all documents that contain an imported copy.

Layouts with Precision

1.12 Creating grid systems is *really* easy with Illustrator.

Illustrator provides you with an ultra-precise drawing and layout environment. Because vectors rely on math to plot the location of each point, putting objects right where you want them is really easy. The object-based drawing model makes each piece of your design accessible and changeable with relative ease. Selecting objects, moving them around, and resizing them happens with laser-like accuracy.

With excellent grid tools and guides, you'll find that creating layouts can happen very quickly (**1.12**). You can create a layout grid (or even multiple grids) in seconds without relying on plug-ins. Smart Guides help you draw with precision, and extensive alignment tools mean you don't have to eyeball where an element lines up with the grid or another object. A broad range of zoom options allows you to get up close and personal in order to work on the minute details. And that's great because, as they say, the devil is in the details.

Conclusion

This chapter skimmed the surface of what makes Illustrator a great tool for UI design. Illustrator is a feature-packed application with many tools designed to help you realize your creative vision.

In the next chapter, you'll get a more in-depth view of Illustrator's tools and workspace. As you continue through the book, my goal is to give you enough knowledge to start using Illustrator right away to create beautiful user interfaces in your own projects.

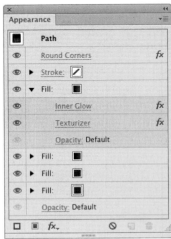

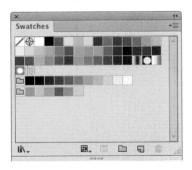

2

TOOLS AND PANELS

Chapter Overview

In the previous chapter, you read a brief overview of the features that make Illustrator a great tool for UI design. In this chapter, we'll take a look at the tools that actually help you get work done. The following topics will be covered:

- How to navigate the Tools panel and find the tools that are useful for UI design tasks
- How to configure and use Illustrator's many panels
- How to use custom workspaces to tailor Illustrator's user interface to the way you work

By the end of the chapter, you should have a basic working knowledge of the main features that Illustrator provides for UI design. Let's begin by jumping right in to the tools.

Choosing Your Tools

Every good design application has a toolbox and, in that department, Illustrator is no slouch. I counted about 85 tools in the Tools panel. For a novice Illustrator user, that seems to be a pretty overwhelming amount of functionality to learn. This is the very reason why professional-grade applications like Illustrator have a relatively steep learning curve.

Thankfully, a UI designer will rarely, if ever, need to use *all* the tools in the Illustrator Tools panel (**2.1**).

Let's cut this huge number of tools down a bit by focusing on the ones that are optimal for UI design. The Tools panel is separated into groups, presumably by functionality or type. Within each of those groups, some tools with similar functions are grouped together under one button. These tool groups are signified with a small arrow in the lower-right corner of the button (**2.2**).

2.2 Click and hold buttons with this icon to reveal the other tools in their respective groups.

2.1 The Illustrator Tools panel

To access hidden tools:

1. Click and hold any button with a small arrow in the lower-right corner. The tool flyout menu appears (**2.3**).

2. To "tear off" the flyout from the main Tools panel, keep the mouse button held down and drag the pointer over the arrow to the right of the flyout and release the mouse button to detach these tools and create a floating tool panel (**2.4**).

    This is convenient if you are focusing on a certain area of your design and don't want to take trips back and forth to the Tools panel. It's also great if you're using one of the hidden tools exclusively.

3. These extra tool panels stay open until you close them. Click the Close button to put the flyout away (**2.5**).

TIP Once you've mastered the basics, take some time to play and experiment with the other tools that aren't covered in this book. Noodling around helps make a beginning user into an intermediate one, and I expect that you'll even find a way to use a tool for a purpose that it wasn't designed. That's ingenuity right there.

2.3 An example of a tool flyout menu

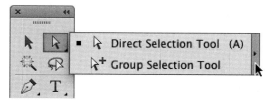

2.4 Click the edge of the flyout to detach it from the Tools panel.

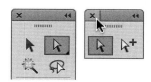

2.5 Click the Close button to put the tool flyout away.

Selection Tools

Right at the top of the Tools panel are five tools for selecting objects. One might say you need only one way to select something, but once you see the flexibility that having multiple options provides, you'll see the reason why there are so many. The selection tool group is made up of the Selection, Direct Selection, Group Selection, Magic Wand, and Lasso tools.

Selection Tool (V)

The Selection tool ![arrow cursor] allows you to pick whole objects with a single click. The Selection tool has the following options:

- Click anywhere on an object to select it. If the object doesn't have a fill, click its edge to select it. You'll know that an entire object is selected when all its points are solid.

- Select multiple objects by holding down the Shift key as you select.

The Bounding Box

As you select an object with the Selection tool, you'll see eight little boxes that surround it (**2.6**), called the bounding box. You can click and drag any of the boxes to resize the object, and hovering the cursor just off a corner will allow you to rotate it. You can choose to show or hide the bounding box from the View menu. The keyboard shortcut is ⌘⇧B/Ctrl+Shift+B.

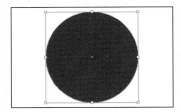

2.6 The bounding box

- Press the ⌘/Ctrl key as you click to select objects behind the topmost object in a stack. As you click, the selection moves down in succession until you reach the bottom.

- Click and drag the Selection tool around an area to select multiple objects. If any part of the object is within the selection box (also known as the selection marquee), that whole object becomes part of the selection (**2.7**).

Direct Selection Tool (A)

The Direct Selection tool 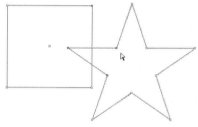 will select an entire object if you click its fill. But the tool goes a step further: It allows you to also select individual points or line segments of an object, which is helpful for reshaping or resizing parts of an object. Select points and segments in the following ways:

- If you can see a point, click it to select it. If you can't see the points, click any line segment on the object to make the points visible. Selected points are solid; unselected points are hollow (**2.8**).

- Add to or remove points from the selection by holding the Shift key as you click.

- Click and drag over multiple points or segments to select them.

- Click a line segment to select it. Unfortunately, you don't get any visual feedback signaling that you have only a segment of the line selected. You have to drag the segment and hope that it's the right one. However, Illustrator is pretty accurate, and it's rare that you'll make an incorrect selection.

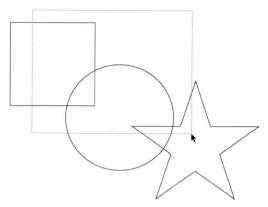

2.7 Drag your cursor over multiple objects to select them all at once.

2.8 Selected points are solid; unselected points are hollow.

Group Selection Tool

Objects in groups are locked together as one. (To group several objects, select the objects and then right-click and choose Group.) Using the regular Selection tool on a group will select the whole group. The Direct Selection tool will still select points and line segments. The Group Selection tool ↖⁺, however, picks individual objects inside the group. To use the Group Selection tool:

- Click an object inside the group to select it. You can then edit the object however you'd like.

- Click again to select the entire group.

Magic Wand Tool (Y)

The Magic Wand tool 🪄 will grab all objects with a specified attribute. For example, if you have a screen full of different colored objects, clicking a red object with the Magic Wand will select all the objects with a red fill. Before you use the Magic Wand tool, though, you can configure how sensitive or tolerant its selection is:

1. In the Tools panel, double-click the Magic Wand tool.

   A panel of options specific to the tool appears (**2.9**).

2. Set the sensitivity of the selection with the Tolerance option. Click the box and type in a value between 0 and 255, or click the arrow to use the slider. A higher number selects a wider range of the chosen attributes.

2.9 Access the Magic Wand panel by double-clicking the Magic Wand tool.

TIP Several of the tools in the Tools panel have configurable settings. Take some time to double-click each of the tools and see what you can find.

Lasso Tool (Q)

The Lasso tool ♖ works a little like the Direct Selection tool in that it allows you to select individual points and segments. The difference is that the Lasso allows you to draw a freeform selection marquee. It also doesn't select the whole object if you click its fill.

To use the Lasso tool, do the following:

1. Click and drag around a point or line segment to select it (**2.10**).

2. Add to the selection by holding the Shift key as you drag around unselected points. You can even select individual points and segments on different objects.

3. Remove points or segments from the selection by holding the Option/Alt key as you drag around selected points.

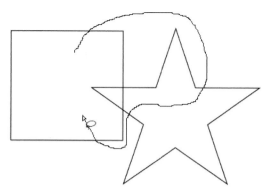

2.10 Selecting a point or line segment

The Select Menu

The Select menu (**2.11**) gives you additional options for making targeted selections. The basic selection options (Select All, Select All on Active Artboard, Deselect, Next Object Above, and Next Object Below) in the menu have keyboard shortcuts. Those are the selection commands you'll use the most often, so I highly recommend learning those shortcuts.

Selecting objects with similar attributes is the real power of this menu. This is an extension of what the Magic Wand tool can do. You can use Select > Same to select any of the following:

- Objects with the same appearance or specific appearance attributes

- All instances of a symbol

- All objects with the same graphic style

Select	Effect	View	Window
All			⌘A
All on Active Artboard			⌥⌘A
Deselect			⇧⌘A
Reselect			⌘6
Inverse			
Next Object Above			⌥⌘]
Next Object Below			⌥⌘[
Same			▶
Object			▶
Save Selection...			
Edit Selection...			

2.11 The Select menu offers powerful selection capabilities.

Drawing

Over the years, Illustrator has become a jack-of-all-trades tool, adept at page layout, illustration, and now website and UI design. In the beginning, however, Illustrator was created for drawing (**2.12**). That's how it got its name. Really, the most useful tools in the Tools panel are probably the drawing tools. These tools provide the means of getting content on the page. There are quite a few drawing tools here; you'll use some more than others.

NOTE This is not a book about learning how to use Illustrator's drawing tools to create illustrations, so it covers only the basics of their use for illustration. For an extensive guide on how to become awesome with Illustrator's drawing tools, I recommend Von Glitschka's excellent book, *Vector Basic Training* (New Riders Press).

2.12 Illustrator was built to create illustrations like this. (The MP3 Effect; © Rick Moore)

Pen Tool (P)

The Pen tool ![pen icon] is probably the tool that most defines Adobe Illustrator. It's a simple tool but a difficult one to master. You use the Pen tool to draw freeform objects in your document point by point. It creates line segments and smooth curves (known formally as Bézier curves). Each curve handle has a control point that allows you to alter the shape of the curve. It's not essential to master the Pen tool to use Illustrator as a UI design tool, but if you want to create anything more than generic shapes, you'll want to take some time to learn how to use it.

First, you'll draw a simple rectangle with the Pen tool.

1. Select the Pen tool and click to set a point.

2. Click to the right of the first point to set another point. The two points are now connected with a line segment (**2.13**).

3. Click to create the third side of the rectangle, and then hover the cursor over the first point you created.

   As you draw, Illustrator's cursor changes to give you helpful feedback. The little circle that appears here means that when you click the starting point, the path will be closed (**2.14**).

Next, you'll draw an ellipse.

1. Click and drag horizontally to set the first curve.

   Illustrator creates a Bézier curve point. Each point in a Bézier curve has one or two control handles that extend from the point itself. You can move these handles to alter the shape of the curve.

2. Click and drag to set three more points (**2.15**). As in the previous exercise, be sure to click the starting point to close the path.

Click and hold the Pen tool to reveal the tools grouped with it (**2.16**). These are the Add Anchor Point tool (+), Delete Anchor Point tool (–), and the Convert Anchor Point tool (Shift-C).

The funny thing about these tools is that, although they are available in the Tools panel, you will never really need to access them there. They are most easily accessed by using keyboard shortcuts while drawing paths with the Pen tool.

2.13 Using the Pen tool to set another point

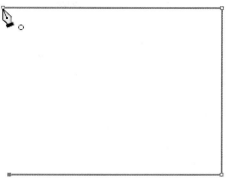

2.14 Click to close the path.

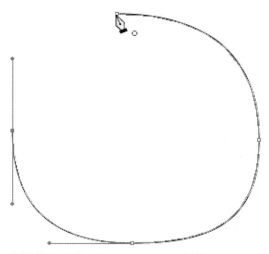

2.15 Click and drag the mouse to create Bézier curves.

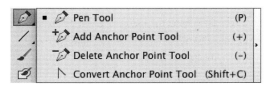

2.16 The Pen tool group

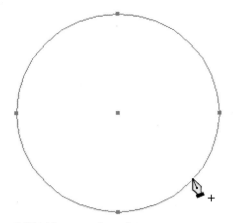

2.17 Adding an anchor point

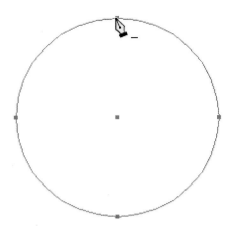

2.18 Deleting an anchor point

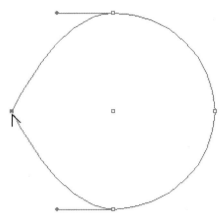

2.19 Converting a smooth point to a corner point

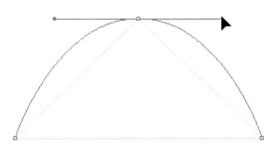

2.20 Converting a corner point to a smooth point

Here's how to access these Point tools while the Pen tool is the active tool:

- Add an anchor point to a path by hovering the cursor over any part of a line segment and clicking. The cursor will change to the Add Anchor Point tool to let you know when you can add a new point (**2.17**).

- Delete an anchor point by hovering the cursor over any point on a path and clicking the point. Again, to provide helpful feedback, the cursor changes to the Delete Anchor Point tool (**2.18**).

- Convert a smooth point to a corner point by holding the Option/Alt key and clicking the point (**2.19**).

- Convert a corner point to a smooth point by holding the Option/Alt key while clicking and dragging Bézier handles out of the point (**2.20**).

Lines and Shapes

Illustrator has several useful tools for creating basic shapes (also known as primitives). These types of shapes will probably be the most useful for UI design. They come in handy as you begin to create icons, buttons, toolbars, menus, and the like.

Line Segment Tool (\)

To create a line segment with the Line Segment tool ✐, do the following:

1. Click to set the starting point.

2. Drag the mouse to draw the segment.

3. Hold the Shift key to constrain the line to the vertical, horizontal, or 45-degree angle axes.

   Use this as an alternative to the Pen tool for creating single lines (also known as rules) in your design.

Rectangle Tool (M)

The Rectangle tool ▣ creates—you guessed it—rectangles. You can click and drag to create a rectangle, or click once to get a dialog box for setting specific parameters.

Ellipse Tool (L)

Click and hold the Rectangle tool to reveal the Ellipse tool ◉. As with the Rectangle tool, when the Ellipse tool is selected, you can click and drag to create an ellipse or click once to get a dialog box for setting specific parameters.

Shape-Drawing Options

The Rectangle and Ellipse tool have keyboard shortcuts to aid in drawing perfect shapes. Both tools allow the following options:

- Use the Shift key while drawing to constrain each shape to a square or circle.

- Hold down the Option/Alt key to draw the shape from the center.

- Hold down the spacebar while drawing to reposition the shape on the artboard.

The Polygon and Star tools (see next page) have shortcuts as well:

- Use the Shift key to lock the rotation angle to 0 degrees as you draw.

- Press the spacebar to move the shape to a different location on the artboard.

- Press the Up or Down arrows on the keyboard to add or remove points from a star and sides from a polygon.

- Press ⌘/Ctrl to change the inner radius of a star.

Polygon and Star Tools

The Polygon and Star tools both reside with the Rectangle tool as well. While these tools are similar to the Rectangle and Ellipse tools in that you can click to set the shape parameters, they have really useful keyboard shortcuts to aid in the creation of interesting shapes. The Star tool is especially useful for creating badges:

1. Click and drag to create a star (**2.21**). The star is always drawn from the center point.

2. Continue to hold the mouse button down and press the Up Arrow key several times. This will add points to the star (**2.22**).

3. When you are satisfied with the number of points, hold down the ⌘/Ctrl key and drag the mouse up to increase the inner radius of the star (**2.23**).

4. Release the mouse button to complete the shape.

2.21 Creating the star

2.22 Adding points to the star

2.23 Changing the inner radius

Typography

Besides being known as a drawing tool, Illustrator also has several tools in its arsenal to help you create professional-level typography. If you're familiar with Adobe InDesign, many of the typographical features in Illustrator work the same way.

Type Tool (T)

The Type tool 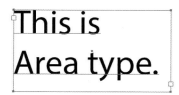 is another very important tool in the Tools panel. It's actually much simpler to use than the Pen tool. Two built-in modes help make this tool really versatile when setting type.

Clicking once in the artboard with the Type tool creates point type (**2.24**). This mode is best for single lines of type or decorative headlines. It has no container, so its length is unconstrained and will stay on one line until you press Enter/Return.

Clicking and drawing a box with the Type tool creates area type (**2.25**). This mode is best for creating long passages. It's also useful when type needs to be constrained to a fixed width without having to rely on hard returns.

The Type tool also has some tools hidden underneath it (**2.26**).

This is Point type.

2.24 Point type is free of any boxes or borders.

This is Area type.

2.25 Area type stays within a user-specified boundary.

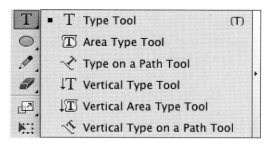

2.26 The Type tool group

Transformation Tools

Illustrator's transformation tools provide easy ways to stretch, resize, rotate, or mirror your design elements.

Reflect Tool (O)

The Reflect tool 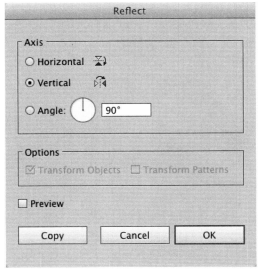, lives under the Rotate tool in the Tools panel. It's used to flip an object on either its vertical or horizontal axis.

1. Option/Alt-click the object to open the Reflect dialog box (**2.27**).

2. Choose Horizontal or Vertical for the axis of reflection. Enter a degree of rotation if desired.

3. Click OK to perform the reflection or click Copy to reflect a copy of the original object.

2.27 The Reflect dialog box

Free Transform Tool (E)

If you have the bounding box turned on (which it is by default), you won't see much of a difference when you select the Free Transform tool from the Tools panel. But while dragging the handles of the bounding box will scale or rotate an object, the Free Transform tool does much more.

It's an extremely versatile tool, and if you're like me, it's probably the one you'll use most often to transform objects. It combines much of the functionality of all the other transformation tools.

TIP If you prefer working with the bounding box turned off, you can use the Free Transform tool (instead of the Scale or Shear tools) to transform an object.

Color

We can't leave color out of the equation, can we? For both the color-loving and the color-challenged, Illustrator has a few powerful color tools in its Tools panel.

Gradient Tool (G)

The Gradient tool ▣ lets you apply multiple colors to a shape or stroke in either a linear or radial fashion. Each gradient has two or more color stops that accept color and opacity. More color stops can be added to create special effects. Gradients can be edited with the Gradient panel (⌘F9/Ctrl+F9) or directly on the object with the gradient annotator.

To create and edit a gradient:

1. Select an object and give it a gradient fill by clicking the Gradient button (>) ▣▣▨ in the Tools panel.

   Illustrator fills in the object with the default gradient, and a bar, called the gradient annotator, appears on top of the object.

2. Adjust the angle and length of the gradient by clicking and dragging across the object.

3. Change the length only by clicking and dragging the square icon on the gradient annotator (**2.28**).

4. Move the gradient around in the object by clicking and dragging the circle end (**2.29**).

5. To rotate the gradient, hover the cursor near the diamond end of the gradient bar. When the cursor changes to the rotation icon, click and drag to rotate (**2.30**).

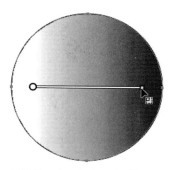

2.28 Changing the length of the gradient

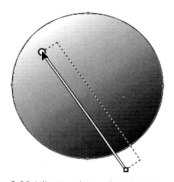

2.29 Adjusting the gradient location

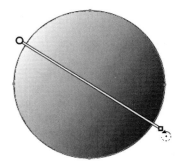

2.30 Rotating the gradient

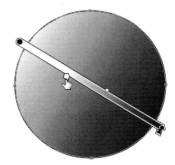

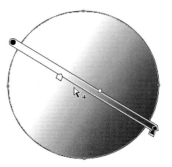

2.31 Adjusting the center point of a gradient

2.32 Dragging color stops across the gradient annotator

2.33 Adding a new color stop

6. Adjust the center point of the gradient by clicking and dragging the center point handle (**2.31**).

7. Adjust color stops by clicking and dragging them across the gradient bar (**2.32**).

8. Each color point on the gradient is called a color stop. Add a new color stop by hovering your cursor just below the gradient bar and then clicking to add the new stop. The cursor will show a plus next to it when you are in the right spot (**2.33**).

9. Change the color stop's value by first double-clicking it.

   The Color panel appears. You'll be able to change the color there (**2.34**).

10. To delete a color stop, click on it and drag it off the gradient bar.

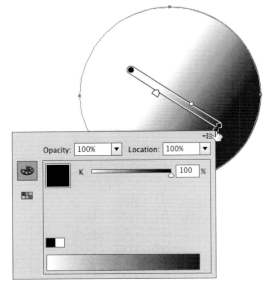

2.34 Using the gradient annotator to change a color stop

Eyedropper Tool (I)

The Eyedropper tool ✐ is used to sample and copy color, type, and effect attributes from one object to another. You can double-click the tool to set selection preferences.

To use the Eyedropper tool:

1. Select the object whose attributes you'd like to change.

2. With the Eyedropper tool, click the object whose attributes you want to copy.

   This will make the selected object look identical by copying all appearance attributes, including any effects.

3. Hold the Shift key to pull (or sample) a color from a portion of a gradient, mesh, or placed image.

2.35 Click the fill or stroke to activate the attribute.

2.36 Clicking this icon will swap the fill and stroke of a selected object.

2.37 Clicking this icon will reset the selected object to the default appearance.

Fill and Stroke

The Fill and Stroke tools display the fill and stroke of the currently selected object. You can click to activate either the fill or stroke by clicking it or toggle between them by pressing X. The active attribute sits on top (**2.35**).

You can swap the fill and stroke of an object by clicking the Swap Fill and Stroke icon (Shift-X) (**2.36**) or reset the object to its default appearance by clicking the Default Fill and Stroke icon (D) (**2.37**). This gives any selected object a white fill and a black stroke. That could come in handy if you've created a mess and want to start from scratch.

Directly below the Fill and Stroke indicators are icons for Color (<), Gradient (>), and None (/) ▣▢▨. These tools give you a quick way to apply the active color or gradient, or remove the fill from a selected object. The icon previews are dynamic for the Color and Gradient options to allow you to see what you will get when you click.

Workspace Tools

The last section of tools contains the Artboard tool ⊡ (Shift-O), the Slice tool 🖊 (Shift-K), the Hand tool ✋ (H), and the Zoom tool 🔍 (Z). These tools are useful for interacting with the workspace itself, and in the case of the Slice tool, for creating areas for exporting artwork. The Slice and Artboard tools aren't covered in detail in this chapter. The functionality they provide warrants much more than a blurb. Instead, look for entire sections devoted to their use in later chapters.

The Hand tool is used to pan and scroll the workspace and can be accessed at any time by pressing the spacebar. Double-clicking the tool in the Tools panel will adjust the view to fit all objects on the selected artboard.

The Zoom tool allows you to zoom in or out of the view (**2.38**). You can either click to adjust the view by 100% increments, or click and drag to specify a spot to magnify. You can access the tool at any time and zoom in by pressing the spacebar and then ⌘/Ctrl. Adding the Option/Alt key will zoom out. Double-clicking the tool will reset the selected artboard to 100%.

2.38 Zooming in with the Zoom tool for close-up work

Modes

The last two sections in the Tools panel control different modes of drawing and viewing artwork.

Drawing Modes

You can use drawing modes to determine how artwork is stacked on the artboard as you draw. Illustrator provides three modes for this purpose. The selected drawing mode stays active until you explicitly turn it off. You can press Shift-D to toggle between modes.

Draw Normal

Draw Normal ⬚⬚⬚ is the default mode and places objects on top of the stack in ascending order as you draw.

Draw Behind

Draw Behind ⬚⬚⬚ places objects at the bottom of the stack in descending order.

Draw Inside

Draw Inside ⬚⬚⬚ provides a quick way to create a mask as it places objects inside of a selected object as you draw. You must select an object to act as the mask before this mode is enabled. Dashed lines on the corners indicate the mask (**2.39**).

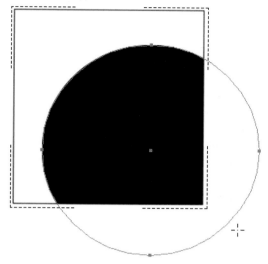

2.39 Draw Inside mode places new objects inside a user-specified shape as you create them.

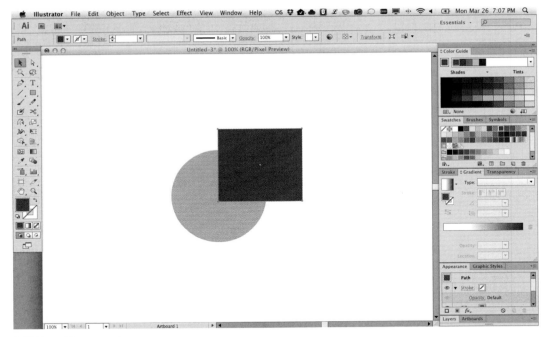

2.40 Normal Screen mode

Screen Modes

The final tool in the Tools panel is the Change Screen Mode tool ⊡ . Screen modes determine how Illustrator's user interface is configured.

To change the screen mode:

1. Click the button to reveal a menu to select the desired screen mode.

2. You can also toggle through screen modes by pressing F.

In Normal Screen mode (**2.40**), your artwork is displayed in a standard window with the menu bar, scroll bars, and panels.

In Full Screen with Menu Bar mode (**2.41**), your artwork window displays full screen.

In Full Screen mode (**2.42**), your artwork displays full screen, and the menu bar, title bar, and all panels are hidden. You can temporarily access the panels by hovering the cursor over the left or right edge of the screen. In any of these modes, pressing Tab will toggle the display of the tools and panels.

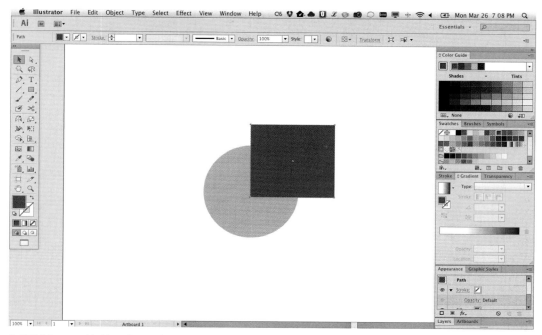

2.41 Full Screen with Menu Bar mode

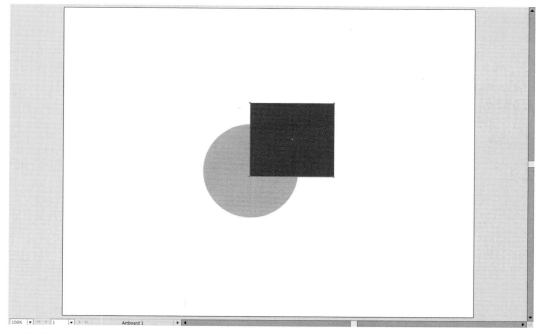

2.42 Full Screen mode

Panels

Illustrator's power lies in the use of onscreen panels. Panels are used to perform tasks like transforming objects, creating and applying colors, organizing artwork, and working with type. They provide an easy way to access this functionality without having to use the menus. Panels also allow you to configure your workspace to suit the task at hand by giving you the option to open or close, dock or float, and expand or collapse functionality on an as-needed basis. Personally, I find that it makes Illustrator easier to use because it enables you to get everything you don't need out of the way and focus on being creative.

Each panel has functionality that is visible in the form of controls, text inputs, and icon buttons. They also have a panel menu at the top right that contains additional functions or options (**2.43**).

2.43 An example of a panel menu

The Control Panel

The Control panel (**2.44**) is the long bar docked to the top of the screen by default. You can dock it to the bottom or just let it float freely as well. I prefer it at the top—it's easier to get the cursor up there. The panel is contextual, which means it displays information based on the currently selected object. You can use the panel menu on the right side of the control panel to choose what information to show.

Illustrator displays this information a couple of different ways, depending on your screen resolution or workspace size. By default, options and preferences are spelled out in detail with input boxes and icons in full view.

2.44 The Control panel

If you're using a smaller display, options that take up the most space are reduced to a link, which pulls down the respective panel when clicked (**2.45**).

Having a lot of panels open takes up precious screen real estate; the Control panel aims to free up some of that space for your artwork by including the functionality of other panels inside of it.

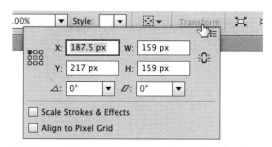

2.45 On smaller screens, some Control panel functionality can be accessed via a link.

Expanding and Collapsing Panels

Panels can be expanded or collapsed to save space in the UI for your artwork. Collapsed panels display as icons (**2.46**). After you click a panel icon, the panel opens and stays open until you close it by clicking its icon again. The downside to using collapsed panels is that you can view only one collapsed panel at a time.

2.46 A collapsed panel group

2.47 Collapsed panels with labels

Panels can be grouped together to form panel groups. Each group has a drag handle at the top and is separated by a line. Clicking and dragging the left edge of the panels reveals the label for each (**2.47**). When you click an icon in a panel group, the panels appear together in tabs with the one you clicked visible. You can switch between tabs by clicking the tab header.

You can move a panel by clicking the drag handle and dragging it to the desired location. As you move a panel, the drop zone is indicated by a blue box. It shows whether the panel will be dropped in between or inside the panel group.

- Drag to a dividing line to place the group between two other groups. Dragging anywhere else will combine the two groups.

- Click and drag the panel icon to move a single panel to another group or to undock it.

- Undock a panel group by clicking the drag handle and pulling it off the edge of the screen. To dock it, drag it back to a dividing line or panel group as in the previous step.

Clicking the double arrow at the top right expands or collapses a panel or panel group (**2.48**). Expanding a panel allows you to view more at once without having to click the icon to open it. Expanded panels take up quite a bit more screen real estate, but the ability to view info at a glance makes the tradeoff worth it.

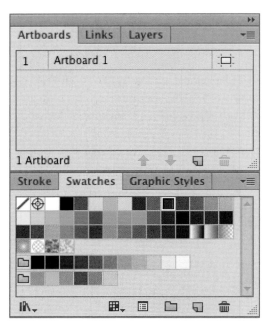

2.48 An expanded panel group

Expanded panels can be moved and docked as well, but the process works a little differently from that of collapsed panels.

- Move a panel group by clicking in the space to the right of the tabs and dragging to the desired location (**2.49**).

- Move a single panel by dragging its tab. To drop it into a different group, drag it to the tab bar of the desired group.

- Change the order of tabs in a group by clicking the tab and dragging it left or right.

- Undock a single panel by dragging its tab off the edge of the screen. Undock a panel group by clicking in the space to the right of the tabs and dragging the edge off the screen. To dock, click and drag the panel bar back to a dividing line or a tab group.

Expanded panels can be collapsed to tabs to allow more space for bigger panels. Collapse to a tab by double-clicking the desired panel's tab. Double-click the tab again to open it. Many panels can be resized by dragging the bottom of the panel.

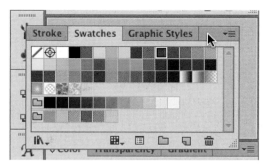

2.49 Moving a panel group

Workspaces

We've only scratched the surface of the functionality that Illustrator offers. One of the awesome features it provides for managing this complexity is the ability to create workspaces that can be customized for a particular task. A workspace is a saved view of the location and position of panels. You can hide or show, dock or free-float, and expand or collapse certain panels and then save them in that state. Illustrator ships with several of these workspaces by default. You can access these workspaces from the workspace switcher at the right of the Application bar, which lives at the top of the screen just above the Control panel (**2.50**).

2.50 The workspace switcher

Using a Custom Workspace

Custom workspaces can be handy when you switch tasks or contexts often. I still do some print work from time to time, so I created a customized print workspace. I also use a laptop hooked to an external display as my primary machine, so I have also created two workspaces that I use depending on whether I am using the large display or the laptop display.

I stated earlier that panels take up a lot of real estate in the interface, so it's important to show only the panels that are completely necessary for the task. I use a mixture of expanded and collapsed panels in my workspace, expanding those I use most often and collapsing those that are "set and forget" panels. Many panels can be left out of the workspace because their functions can be accessed from within other panels.

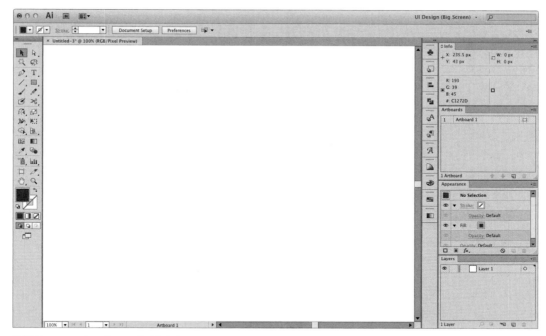

2.51 My personal workspace for UI design

I set up a custom workspace that I find optimum for UI design (**2.51**).

Here is how it's set up:

The Application frame (covered in Chapter 3, "The Illustrator Workspace") is enabled. This keeps me from accidentally clicking windows in the background.

On the right, I have a group of collapsed panels that represent functionality I use often, but not enough to need to see them all the time. From top to bottom they are:

- Symbols
- Graphic Styles
- Align
- Pathfinder
- Character Styles
- Paragraph Styles
- Glyphs
- Color Guide
- Color
- Swatches
- Gradient

To the right of the collapsed panel group is a group of expanded panels that I rely on for constant information and interaction. Again, from top to bottom they are as follows:

- Info
- Artboards
- Appearance
- Layers

As you learn to use Illustrator, you'll find a workspace configuration that works for you. That's one of the great things about Illustrator: It gives you the flexibility to work the way you need it to, rather than the other way around. As you create your own workspaces, it's best to restart Illustrator to ensure that your layout is saved. If you don't perform this step, you'll lose this workspace if Illustrator ever crashes.

Creating a new workspace may seem like a lot of work, but thankfully you'll have to do it only once for each context. You can easily change your workspaces as the task or context changes. This is one of the keystones to efficiency that I cover throughout the book.

If you need to rename or delete a custom workspace, you can do that by choosing Manage Workspaces from the workspace switcher.

Conclusion

We've covered a lot of ground in this chapter, and I hope you've gained a basic working knowledge of the tools and functions needed to start creating great designs. In the next chapter, you'll learn how to set up Illustrator for working with pixels instead of print documents and how to use artboards to maximize efficiency in the creation of UI screens.

TABLE 2.1 Keyboard Shortcuts in This Chapter

	MAC OS	WINDOWS
Selection tool	V	V
Direct Selection tool	A	A
Magic Wand tool	Y	Y
Lasso tool	Q	Q
Pen tool	P	P
Line Segment tool	\	\
Rectangle tool	M	M
Ellipse tool	L	L
Type tool	T	T
Reflect tool	O	O
Free Transform tool	E	E
Gradient tool	G	G
Fill or stroke object with gradient	>	>
Fill or stroke with color	<	<
Remove fill or stroke	/	/
Eyedropper tool	I	I
Fill/Stroke toggle	X	X
Swap Fill/Stroke	⇧X	Shift+X
Default Fill/Stroke	D	D
Drawing mode toggle	⇧D	Shift+D
Screen mode toggle	F	F

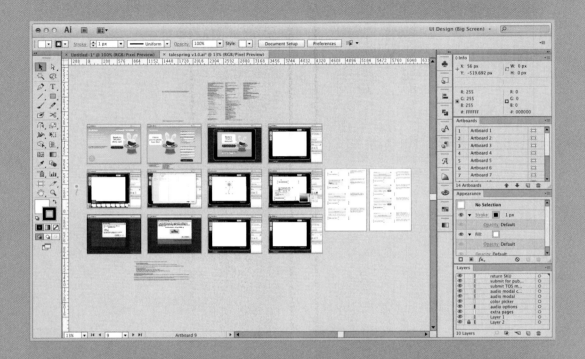

THE ILLUSTRATOR WORKSPACE

Chapter Overview

In this chapter, you'll learn about the following:

- Choosing the right measurement units
- Selecting the optimal color space
- Creating artboards and organizing your work

The Adobe Illustrator workspace is designed to allow you to be as creative as you want without a lot of distractions. It has a generous area for creating your designs and minimal user interface chrome. The workspace is very flexible and can be customized to your liking.

Go from Print to Pixels

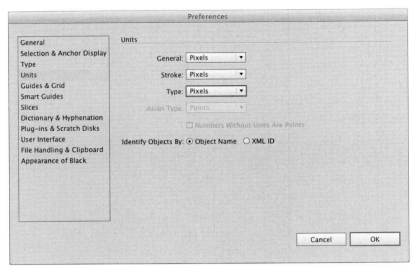

3.1 Setting the General, Stroke, and Type units to pixels

As you already know, this is a book about designing for the screen, whether your target user platform is a laptop or desktop screen, tablet screen, smartphone screen, or TV screen. But out of the box, Illustrator is set up for working with print documents. You'll need to make some adjustments so that it's more appropriate for screen graphics.

Choosing the Right Units

The first option to modify is Illustrator's unit of measure. In the print world, measurements are usually picas and points, inches, millimeters, or a combination of those. However, in UI design, pixel measurements should be the standard. Illustrator can be adjusted so that you can view everything, including type, with pixel measurements.

This setting will help your documents more accurately reflect what end users will view on their devices. Fortunately, this is simple to change.

1. Choose Illustrator > Preferences > Units (Mac) or Edit > Preferences > Units (Windows).

   The Preferences dialog box appears (**3.1**).

2. Change the unit definitions for General, Stroke, and Type to Pixels.

Optimizing the Color Space

The second thing to take care of is changing Illustrator's color profile. Again, by default, this is set up with a profile that works best in a printing environment. You might easily justify leaving this setting alone, since no

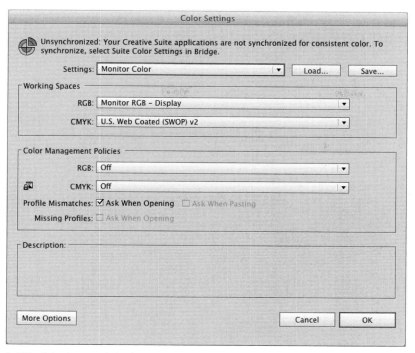

3.2 The Color Settings dialog box

two screens are alike in how they show color, but you'll change it in case you ever want to edit your design in Photoshop or incorporate images from Photoshop.

1. Choose Edit > Color Settings (⌘⇧K/ Ctrl+Shift+K) to access the Color Settings dialog box (**3.2**).

2. In the Settings pop-up menu, choose Monitor Color.

NOTE If you plan to shuttle graphics back and forth to Photoshop, you'll want to make the same change there so the two apps are in sync. By doing so, you eliminate surprise color changes.

Application Frame

The Illustrator workspace may look a little different depending on which platform you are running. If you're using a Windows PC, you will see the tools and default panel configuration running in a window. On a Mac, however, the tools and panels float freely on the screen. Some Mac users prefer this behavior— it's what we're used to with all the other apps we use. However, I've actually come to like the Application frame (shown in **3.3** and **3.4**) because it reduces distractions from underlying windows. I've found myself clicking a window in the background far too often to count. If you want to give the Application frame a try, simply turn it on by choosing Window > Application Frame.

3.3 If you run a lot of applications in the background on a regular basis, the standard Mac configuration has the potential to get messy.

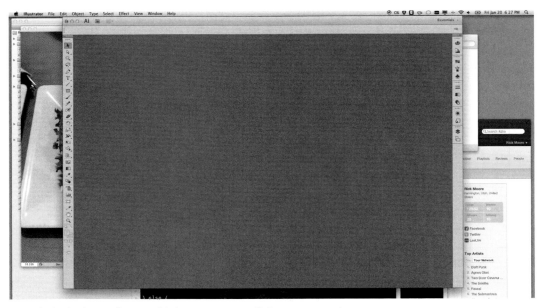

3.4 With the Application frame enabled, you can more easily focus on your task.

Working with Artboards

Artboards are a unique and powerful feature of Illustrator. The artboard works just like a piece of paper would on a physical desk. For example, if you were creating a collage, you could put elements you are not currently using on your desk outside of the bounds of the paper. They are still close for easy access, but they don't interfere with the artwork taking shape on the document. Illustrator works in a similar way.

When you create a new document, you have an artboard in the middle of a large workspace. Any graphics you place on the artboard itself will appear in the final design. Anything outside its bounds will not appear when you print, export, or save as a PDF. It's a great way to keep all of your assets in one file rather than scattered across separate files on your hard disk, or in hidden layers that become hard to manage.

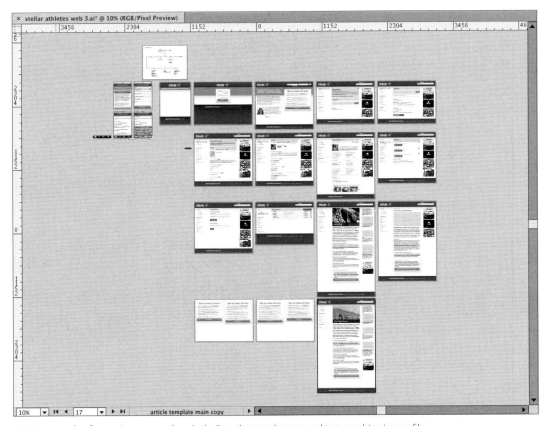

3.5 An example of an entire app mockup, including alternate layouts and test graphics, in one file.

What's even better is that you can have multiple artboards in one Illustrator document. Illustrator allows you to create up to 100 artboards in a file, depending on the size of the artboards used. You can use these extra artboards to create a site map, show different states of an interaction, or test several design options for a particular screen (**3.5**). Additionally, it makes it a lot easier to create multi-page PDFs for client reviews and presentations.

However you end up using artboards, I'm sure you'll find them very powerful when creating user interfaces. You can keep an entire site in one file and make managing all your design assets so much easier.

Opening a New Document

Let's create a new document to check out all that the workspace has to offer.

1. Choose File > New (⌘N/Ctrl+N).

   You'll see a dialog box that has options for your new document (**3.6**). Here you'll have the opportunity to name your file and choose a profile. Illustrator has several built-in profiles for you to use as a starting point.

2. Select the Web profile.

   Notice several differences between the Web and Print profiles: The document units are pixels instead of points, and the preset artboard dimensions are 960 px by 560 px, a common viewable area for a browser window. You can use one of the presets or type your own dimensions in the width and height fields.

3. Click the triangle to the left of the Advanced section to open it (**3.7**).

   This section of the dialog box is where you can set the color mode (CMYK or RGB), screen resolution for raster effects (we'll look at how to use these effects in a later chapter), and preview mode for the document.

   The next two settings are ones that I have found to be very useful for UI design.

4. Change Preview Mode to Pixel.

   Pixel preview displays your art as if it was created with pixels rather than vector objects. It shows how your artwork will be anti-aliased when viewed at 72 ppi, which is the resolution graphics will be when exported from the program. You'll feel really comfortable in this mode if you're used to working in Photoshop.

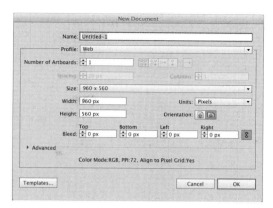

3.6 The New Document dialog box

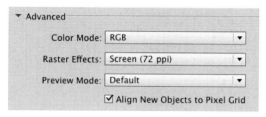

3.7 Advanced artboard options

5. Leave "Align New Objects to Pixel grid" checked and click OK.

This feature keeps your artwork aligned to the pixel grid as you draw. That way, your art stays crisp when saving your graphics for the web or devices.

NOTE See page 80 for more on pixel precision.

Saving New Profiles

The profiles included with Illustrator are limited to some of the most popular devices on the market today. Notably missing from the list is the iPhone 4 and iPad with their retina display resolutions. If the iPhone's 640 x 960 is a screen size you use often, you can create your own profile:

1. Create a new document and use 640 x 960 as the dimensions.

2. On a Mac, save your document to Hard Drive:Users:[user name]:Library:Application Support:Adobe:Adobe Illustrator CS6:[language]:New Document Profiles. In Windows, save your file to C:\Documents and Settings\[user name]\Application Data\ Adobe\Adobe Illustrator CS6 Settings\[language]\New Document Profiles.

If you're a Mac OS X Lion user, you'll find that the Library folder is hidden. To access it, perform the following steps:

1. Open a new window from the Finder.

2. Open the Go menu on the menu bar, and then press the Option key. Your Library folder will magically appear.

3. Click the Library folder to open it, and then drag it to the sidebar in the Finder window. Now when you save a file, you'll have easy access to the Library.

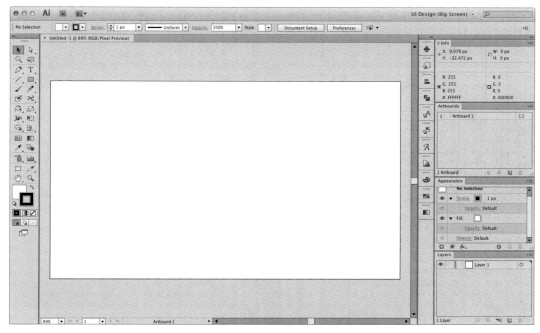

3.8 Hello, artboard!

Creating Artboards

Behold the white rectangle in the middle of the screen (**3.8**). This, my friend, is the artboard. Illustrator uses this metaphor as its working space. As I stated previously, the artboard is really just like a piece of paper sitting on your desk. You can draw on it, paint it, erase stuff from it, and move it around. At times I think Adobe should add the ability to crumple it up and toss it into the wastebasket, but I digress…

For those of you coming from Photoshop, the artboard is fundamentally different from Photoshop's canvas. First of all, it's another vector object on the screen you can edit without affecting the artwork itself. You can resize it, change its orientation, duplicate it, and remove it. It's pretty versatile.

Second, the artboard acts a container for your design, allowing you to place unneeded elements outside its bounds without having to delete them or toss them into hidden layers. Anything outside the artboard bounds stays out of your printed or exported files. This enables you to experiment with different ideas outside the artboard before you decide to include them in the final artwork.

As for multiple artboards, I think it's one of the best features Illustrator has to offer. It makes mocking up entire sites very easy and keeping your entire project in one place really helps with efficiency. When working on enterprise sites that have multiple layers of functionality, I tend to break up modules into different files. I've created upwards of 50 screens in one file with no discernible hit on performance and a relatively small file size.

There are several ways to create a new artboard that go beyond opening a new document. Let's take a look at how you can do this in the next few sections.

The Artboard Tool (Shift-O)

In the Tools panel is a dedicated tool called the Artboard tool (Shift-O) ⬜. Activating the Artboard tool puts Illustrator into artboard editing mode. Once activated, the artboard has a bounding box, grab handles, crop marks, and a nameplate appearing with it in the workspace (**3.9**). You have a couple of options in this mode:

- Add a new artboard by clicking and dragging the cursor anywhere outside the current artboard. This allows you to create an artboard of any size. If you need to change the size, just click and drag any of the grab handles to adjust. This works for any artboard in the workspace.

- Delete an artboard by selecting it and pressing Delete. If you have multiple artboards to eradicate, pressing Delete multiple times will remove them in descending order until you have only one left.

  One thing to note is that Illustrator requires at least one artboard at all times. Additionally, deleting the artboard does not delete the art on it. You have to do that manually.

3.9 Crop marks, bounding box handles, and a nameplate are all visible in artboard editing mode.

TIP To make the artboard larger than the current window while resizing, drag the cursor to the edge of the screen and it will automatically scroll to reveal more space.

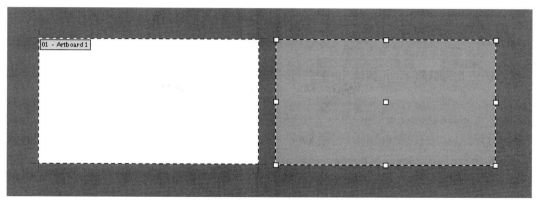

3.10 Click to place a new artboard.

Using the Control Panel

The Control panel has several tools within it for dealing with artboards. Because the panel is contextual, you'll need to be in artboard editing mode to view these tools. You can perform the following actions from the Control panel:

- Set the selected artboard to a preset size

- Change the orientation to portrait or landscape

- Add a new artboard

- Delete a selected artboard

- Name a selected artboard

- Choose whether to have artwork move with the artboard when it is rearranged

- Show extras like crosshairs, video-safe rulers, and a center mark

- Show the Artboard Options dialog box

- Place or resize an artboard with numerical precision

To use the Control panel to create a new artboard, do the following:

1. Click the Artboard tool (Shift-O) to enter artboard editing mode.

2. Create a new artboard by clicking the New Artboard icon ▣ in the Control panel.

   This allows you to place a new artboard in the workspace that's the same size and orientation as the currently selected artboard. After clicking the New Artboard icon, you'll notice that you have a box that follows the cursor (**3.10**).

3. Click anywhere in the workspace to place the new artboard in that spot.

Using the Artboards Panel

The Artboards panel (**3.11**) shows you a list of all artboards in your document. Unlike the Control panel, it is available at any time. Create a new artboard with the Artboard panel by clicking the New Artboard icon at the bottom of the panel.

Illustrator will put new artboards created this way to the right of the current artboard. If you have several rows of artboards, it will always place the new artboard to the far right of the top row. This gets tricky as you start to create a lot of artboards, as Illustrator won't let you place artboards outside the workspace.

You can also perform the following actions from the Artboards panel:

- Select an artboard as the active artboard
- Double-click an artboard in the list to view it in the window
- Move an artboard up or down in the page flow by dragging in the list or using the arrows at the bottom of the panel
- Delete an active artboard
- Rename an artboard

The panel menu also allows you to duplicate or rearrange artboards, convert objects to artboards, and delete empty ones.

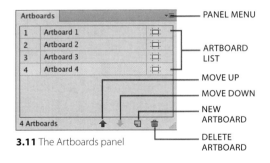

3.11 The Artboards panel

Duplicating an Artboard

Duplicating an artboard can save you time by giving you a quick start on a new screen where most of the elements are the same. This is useful if you are trying to show different interaction states for an element or just want to try a different color scheme for the same design. There are a couple of easy ways to accomplish this:

1. Select the Artboard tool (Shift-O).

2. In the Control panel, make sure that the "Move/Copy Artwork with Artboard" option is selected. If this is option is deselected, you will only duplicate the artboard itself.

3. Click the artboard you'd like to clone and hold the Option/Alt key as you drag it to a new location. To constrain the artboard to the horizontal or vertical axis, hold the Shift key, too.

   You can also use the Artboards panel to duplicate an artboard by selecting the one you want to clone and dragging it to the New Artboard icon (**3.12**). It will place the duplicated artboard using the same rules outlined in the previous section.

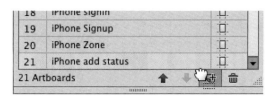

3.12 Drag an artboard in the list to the New Artboard icon to create a duplicate.

Using Existing Objects

In addition to creating new, blank artboards, you can use an existing object as the basis for a new artboard. This is useful in several common scenarios:

- You have design elements outside of a current artboard that you want to move to a new artboard.

- You want to move a part of your design to a new artboard *and* create the new artboard at the same time.

- You want to quickly export or create a PDF of part of your design.

To create a new artboard from an existing object, perform the following steps:

1. Select the Artboard tool (Shift-O).

2. Click the object you want to use as the basis for the new artboard (**3.13**).

   Once you've done this, you can resize or rearrange the new artboard like you would any other.

3.13 Click an existing object with the Artboard tool to create a new artboard based on its boundaries.

Organizing Artboards

Once you get several artboards in your document, things might have a tendency to get a little messy. Missing artboard names, disorganized screens, and holes in the screen flow drive me crazy. If that bothers you like it does me, it's pretty easy to get everything back in shape.

Give Them Names

You might have noticed that as you add new artboards to your document, each one gets a generic name, such as Artboard 1, Artboard 2, and so on. As convenient as this is, it isn't really helpful as your project grows. It's akin to a Photoshop document with a plethora of unnamed layers. To deal with this problem, Illustrator allows you to name your artboards (**3.14**).

1. Select the Artboard tool (Shift-O) and select the artboard you want to name.

2. Type a new name in the Name field in the Control panel. Making the name relevant to the content on the artboard will help immensely as you add more artboards to your project.

You can also use the Artboards panel to name your artboards.

•   Select the artboard you want to name in the panel list and then click its Artboard icon once. The Artboard Options dialog box appears, where you can type the new name as well as access various other options.

3.14 Name your artboards for maximum efficiency.

Move Them Around

When I work on a large project, I typically start with a set number of artboards. As I work through the design process, I organize the artboards into a flow or site map. As features and functionality gets added or removed, the number of screens needed in the mockup may grow or shrink. When this happens, I end up with screens that are out of order or have holes in the flow (**3.15** and **3.16**). To fix this problem, Illustrator allows the ability to rearrange artboards in the workspace.

To move artboards manually, do the following:

1. With the Artboard tool (Shift-O), click the artboard you wish to move and drag it around the workspace until you have it in the desired position.

2. If you want to leave the art where it is and move just the artboard, make sure to deselect the "Move/Copy Artwork with Artboard" icon .

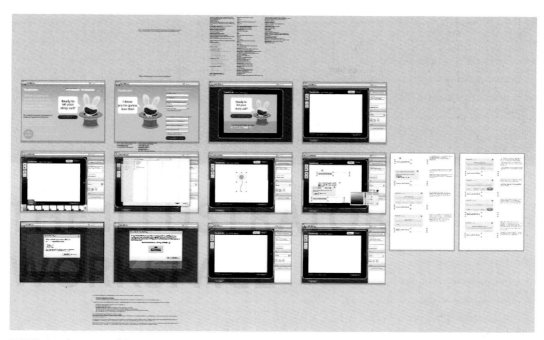

3.15 During the course of designing a UI…

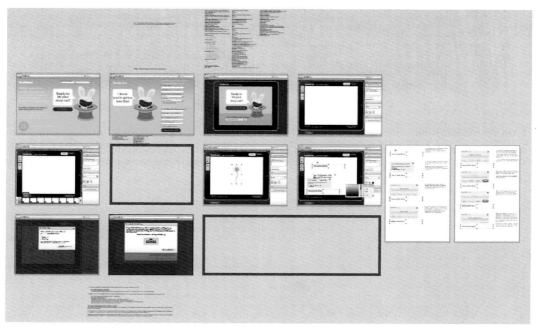

3.16 …pages sometimes get removed, leaving holes in the page flow.

To rearrange artboards using the Artboards panel:

1. Make sure that your artboards are in the order you'd like them to flow in the workspace by dragging them into position in the panel (**3.17**). The number next to the artboard in the panel corresponds to its position in the workspace.

2. From the Artboards panel menu, choose Rearrange Artboards.

3. Choose the layout you prefer, how many columns to use, and the desired space between each artboard (**3.18**). If you don't have "Move Artwork with Artboard" selected in the Control panel, don't worry. You can select it here so that all of your art gets rearranged as well. Click OK.

After a second or so, you'll see the workspace zoom to fit all the artboards and you'll see them in their new positions.

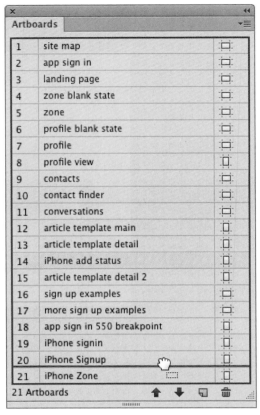

3.17 Drag artboards to order them the way you'd like them to appear in the workspace.

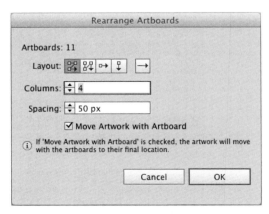

3.18 The Rearrange Artboards dialog box

Navigating Multiple Artboards

Once you have a few artboards in the workspace, you'll need an easy way to move between them. You could use the scrollbars or the Hand tool to scroll the workspace, but that's slow and imprecise. Instead, you can use the Artboards panel or the artboard navigator to quickly and easily find the right artboard.

To switch artboards through the Artboards panel:

- Double-click the desired artboard in the panel. It jumps into view on the screen at whatever zoom percentage it needs to fit the whole artboard in the window. To reset the zoom level to 100%, double-click the Zoom tool or press ⌘1/Ctrl+1.

The artboard navigator (**3.19**) is found at the bottom-left corner of the document window. To use the artboard navigator:

- Choose the desired artboard from the pop-up menu (**3.20**). This is so much easier if you named your artboards.

- Use the Next and Previous buttons to click through a series of screens in succession.

    This succession is determined by the order of the artboards in the Artboards panel. Clicking the Next and Previous arrows moves one screen at a time, while clicking the First and Last arrows jumps to the first and last artboards.

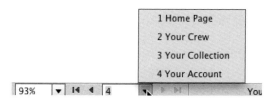

3.19 The artboard navigator

3.20 Your artboard list

If you just need to move around a particular area in the workspace or artboard (for example, if you are zoomed in doing close-up work), you can use the Hand tool (H) 🖐:

1. Select the Hand tool (H). You can click and drag around the workspace until you choose another tool.

2. To quickly access the Hand tool while using another tool, press and hold the spacebar. You'll be able to pan around the workspace as long as you have the spacebar pressed. When you let go, you will return to the tool you had previously been using.

Conclusion

Artboards are one of my favorite features in Illustrator. They allow for convenience in creating and organizing your artwork. Being able to keep multiple screens in one document, visualize interaction flows, or mock up a workflow process is invaluable and will help you work efficiently.

The next chapter looks at using the pixel grid to preview how changes in anti-aliasing affect your design. Even when creating UIs for high-resolution devices like the iPhone and iPad, having pixel-precise measurements will make your developers love you as they work to match your design.

The next chapter also looks at how to use Illustrator for basic UI design tasks like setting up grids and working with typography.

TABLE 3.1 Keyboard Shortcuts in This Chapter

	MAC	PC
Color Settings	⌘⇧K	Ctrl+Shift+K
New Document	⌘N	Ctrl+N
Artboard tool	⇧O	Shift+O
Hand tool	H	H
Actual Size	⌘1	Ctrl+1

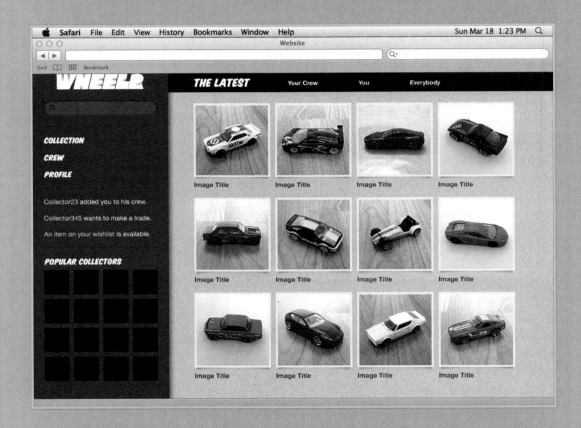

4

UI DESIGN BUILDING BLOCKS

Chapter Overview

Up to this point, we've spent some time getting to know Illustrator's user interface. Now it's time to begin putting those tools into action and start creating a UI yourself. This chapter takes a look at the basic features that Illustrator provides for the building blocks of UI design:

- Using guides and alignment tools
- Creating page grids
- Achieving pixel precision
- Beginning a layout
- Setting type

You'll learn these features in the context of creating a screen for a mock web application for die-cast car collectors. The mockup has several elements: a sidebar that contains the app name, a search field, app navigation, and some activity info. It also has a section navigation bar and a main content area. It has some simulated browser chrome to finish it off. I'll show you how to create this over the next few chapters.

Guides Objectified

Every professional design application lets you set guides to help you align objects in your document. Alignment is one of the design principles that make any design just feel right. It brings cohesiveness into the layout. In Illustrator, there are two basic ways to use guides in your documents:

- Create an ad-hoc guide when you need to align several objects to a certain plane.

- Pull several guides out to create a layout grid.

By default, guides are "magnetic." Dragging an object will cause it to snap to a guide once it gets within a certain pixel distance (**4.1**). This ensures that your objects will line up exactly as you want them. Alternatively, dragging a guide to a selected object will snap the guide to that object.

Guides will be helpful in the mockup for aligning graphic elements. You'll explore Illustrator's guides by first creating a new document for the mockup:

1. Choose File > New. In the dialog box, choose the Web profile.

2. Select 1024 x 768 as the artboard size and click OK to create the document.

    This size represents the target display resolution you'll use for this mockup.

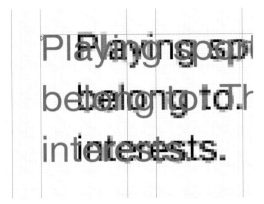

4.1 The drag cursor changes to white when an object has snapped to a guide.

Creating Guides

Now that you have a document open, it's time to create some guides. In order to create guides, you'll need to make sure your rulers are visible. If they aren't showing at the top and left side of the document window, choose View > Rulers > Show Rulers (⌘R/Ctrl+R).

1. Click and drag a guide from the ruler onto the artboard.

2. If you didn't get the guide in just the right spot, undo the guide placement by doing *one of the following:*

   • Press ⌘Z/Ctrl+Z to undo the guide placement and try again.

   • Move the guide into place by selecting it and dragging until you have it positioned correctly. If you are unable to move the guide, it may be locked. Choose View > Guides > Lock Guides (⌘⌥; [semicolon]/Ctrl+Alt+; [semicolon]) to unlock the guides. Selecting this menu option toggles the lock state on or off.

3. To remove a guide, simply select it and press Delete (make sure the guide is unlocked).

4. If you no longer need any guides in your document, or need to start over, remove them all at once by choosing View > Guides > Clear Guides.

NOTE Guides are always visible by default; you can choose to show or hide guides as well. To do so, choose View > Guides > Hide Guides (⌘;/Ctrl+;) to toggle guide visibility. If your guides are hidden, the menu changes to read Show Guides.

Making Guides from Objects

Another awesome feature is the ability to make any vector object on the artboard into a guide. This is really helpful if you need to align objects at strange angles. This feature has a practical use:

1. Click and drag with the Line tool (\) and draw a line on the artboard.

2. Select the line and choose View > Guides > Make Guides (⌘5/Ctrl+5).

   You object is instantly turned into a guide, taking on all current attributes you have set for your guides (such as snapping behavior, visibility, lock state, and color). This is a great way to align objects already on your artboard to an angle without having to measure (**4.2**).

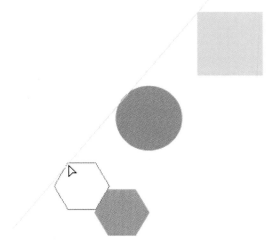

4.2 Snapping an object to a custom guide

You can also convert any guide—whether you pulled it from a ruler or created it from an object—into an object:

1. Make sure that guides are unlocked (⌘⌥; [semicolon]/Ctrl+Alt+; [semicolon]). You won't be able to select them otherwise.

2. Select the guide you want to convert and choose View Guides > Release Guides (⌘⌥5/Ctrl+Alt+5).

   The guide is now an object, selected and ready for you to work with.

Using Alignment Tools

Besides allowing you to snap and align objects to guides, Illustrator also provides powerful alignment features accessible via the Align panel (Shift-F7). This panel (**4.3**) helps to align objects to an axis or position as well as distribute them across a distance. A few of the more commonly used alignment features can also be accessed in the Control panel when you have more than one object selected.

The buttons in the top row of the Align panel align objects by their edges and centers along the horizontal and vertical axes. The buttons provide a graphical representation of how Illustrator will align the selected objects.

The buttons in the bottom row of the panel distribute objects across a distance based on the axis or edge that the user has chosen. This is very different from aligning objects. Instead of lining them up along a single edge or center, Illustrator will equally space the objects from the edge or center you clicked.

You can make a couple of extra options (**4.4**) visible by choosing Show Options from the Align panel menu. The first of these options, Distribute Spacing, distributes objects across a distance by putting an equal amount of space (which can be user-specified) between them.

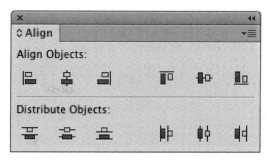

4.3 The Align panel

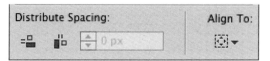

4.4 Align Panel extra options

The second button houses the Align To options. These options allow you to choose how objects will align in the following ways:

- **To the selection (the default behavior):** The selection in this option represents the area in which all selected objects are contained. For example, if you have four rectangles and you want to align all of their left edges, clicking the align left button would move all but the leftmost rectangle.

- **To the artboard:** This option aligns objects to centers or edges of the artboard itself. This alignment method is best used when you want to center a single object or a selection of objects on the artboard.

- **To a key object:** This option allows you to select an object to which all other objects in the selection will align. This method is best used when the object you want to align to needs to stay in place.

To designate an object in your selection as the key object, perform the following steps:

1. Select all objects (including the one that will be the key object) you want to align either by dragging a selection box around them or by Shift-clicking each object.

2. Set the key object for the selection by clicking it.

   The key object is always indicated by a bold selection outline (**4.5**).

4.5 The key object is indicated by a bold selection outline.

Smart Guides

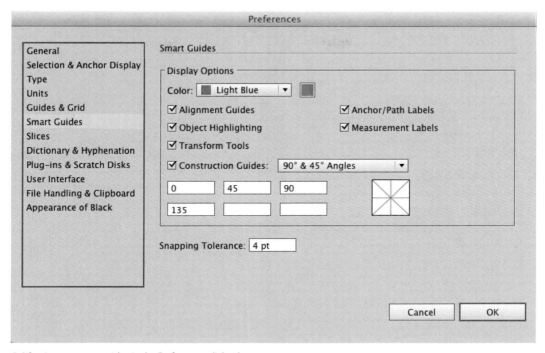

4.6 Setting up smart guides in the Preferences dialog box

Illustrator has another type of guide called a Smart Guide. Instead of being just a static object to which you can align something, smart guides are dynamic and provide useful feedback as you draw. There are six different types of Smart Guides you can set up in the Preferences dialog box (**4.6**). You can enable as many of these guides as you'd like, or disable them altogether. You may find it a little intrusive to have these guides on all the time; you can toggle the guides on or off by choosing View > Smart Guides (⌘U/Ctrl+U).

What follows is a description of how each type of Smart Guide works. Play around with each of the settings to see which ones work best for your workflow.

Alignment Guides

Alignment guides help you to align objects while drawing, moving, or editing. They help you align objects and anchor points to the centers and/or edges of nearby objects (**4.7**) without having to pull guides from the ruler.

Anchor/Path Labels

Anchor/path labels appear as you hover over an object to let you know whether you have an anchor point, path, center point, or edge of an object under your cursor. This really aids in making selections once you have a more complex design (**4.8**).

Object Highlighting

With the Object Highlighting Smart Guide enabled, objects are highlighted with a selection outline as you hover over them. Again, this Smart Guide is most useful when you have a lot of objects on the artboard, as it allows you a preview of what object will be selected when you click. It also allows you to see objects that have live effects applied, as seen in **4.9**.

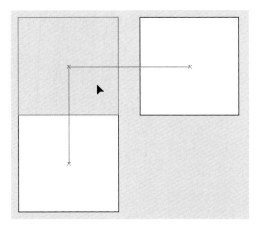

4.7 Using alignment guides helps align objects as you move them around.

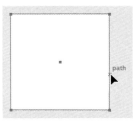

4.8 Anchor/path labels let you know what's beneath your cursor.

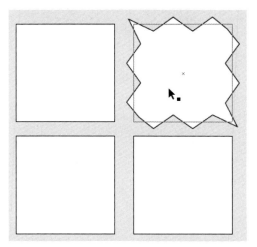

4.9 Object highlighting shows which object will be selected when you click. It also shows the original shape of objects with effects applied to them.

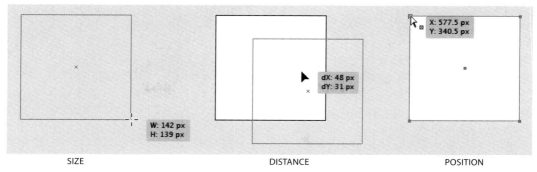

SIZE DISTANCE POSITION

4.10 Measurement labels provide in-context information about the dimensions and position of objects.

Measurement Labels

Measurement labels display the size, distance, and position of objects as you draw, move, or edit them (**4.10**). It helps you to be really precise with layout and placement in context.

Transform Tools

Transform tools display guides when used with the Rotate, Scale, or Shear tools (**4.11**). These guides help to constrain these transformations to common angles when drawing, so you don't have to use the Shift key to do the same thing.

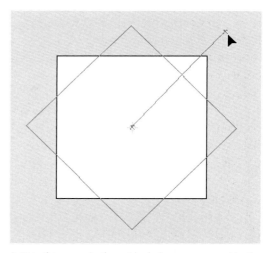

4.11 In this example, the guides help you snap an object's rotation to 45-degree angles.

Construction Guides

When drawing with the Pen tool, construction guides help to constrain line segments to specified angles (**4.12**). You can choose a preset angle group or specify your own custom angles (see 4.6).

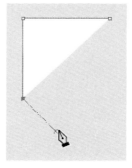

4.12 Construction guides make drawing with the Pen tool a little easier.

Grids Made Easy

Over the last several years much discussion has taken place about using traditional grids in web design. Articles and books by designers like Mark Boulton and Khoi Vinh have helped us learn and understand how to use grids effectively to create beautiful designs for the screen. Constraints in design can be a pain and a blessing at the same time. Creating a grid is an essential task that will enable a foundation on which to build a consistent design scheme.

How do we create grids today? I'm sure designers everywhere use a lot of different methods, including not using a grid at all. Typically, though, we painstakingly create a grid by dragging guides from rulers and trying to place them consistently on the page.

My old process for creating a grid was ridiculous. I used to draw a couple of rectangles, one for the column width and one for the gutter, and then copy and paste them end to end across the page. I'd use those as markers

Grid Resources

Here are links to a two really good resources on designing grids for the web:

- "Simple Steps to Designing Grid Systems" by Mark Boulton: http://d.pr/OkyC

- *Ordering Disorder: Grid Principles for Web Design* (*New Riders Press, 2010*) by Khoi Vinh: http://d.pr/m6yZ

so that I would know where to snap my guides. Every new page I would create would need to use the grid; worse, I would often have multiple files or grid layers on sites that called for the use of more than one grid. If those grids ended up changing, frustration would ensue.

Fuss no more, as Illustrator can help make you more productive by not only letting you create a single grid easily, but also allowing you to maintain multiple grids in a single document.

Creating a Grid

You'll start the mockup for Wheelr by creating a standard 950 pixel-wide grid with 24 columns and 10-pixel gutters. This grid will sit in the center of the 1024 x 768 document you created earlier, defining the "safe" area in a browser or tablet device. In the past, I would have done all kinds of math (which I'm no good at) to figure out how wide the columns and gutters needed to be so that the measurements were in whole numbers. Thankfully, there is a feature in Illustrator that will do these tricky calculations automatically.

1. Start by choosing View > Guides > Clear Guides to remove all the guides. This will give you a clean slate from which to begin.

4.13 Center the rectangle on the artboard before you create the grid.

2. Draw a 950 (W) x 768 (H) rectangle, give it a color of your choosing, and align it to the center of the artboard (**4.13**) using the Align to Artboard feature.

3. Choose Object > Path > Split Into Grid.

   The resulting dialog box allows you to choose settings for this particular grid.

4. Under the Columns section, enter *24* in the Number field and *10 px* in the Gutter field (**4.14**).

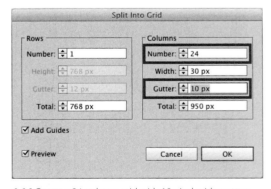

4.14 Create a 24-column grid with 10 pixel-wide gutters.

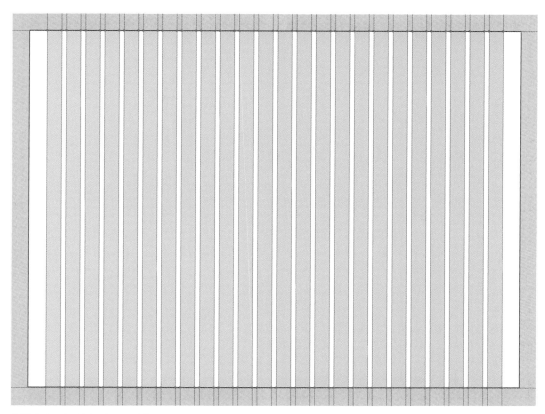

4.15 A standard 24-column grid.

5. Select the Preview option to see what's being created, and select the Add Guides option so you don't have to add your guides manually afterwards. Click OK.

   The rectangle you started with is now divided into 24 rectangles (**4.15**). The grid and the rectangles should all be selected at this point.

6. Press and hold the Shift key and click the guides to deselect them.

7. The extra rectangles are unnecessary at this point, so press Delete to get rid of them.

NOTE When creating the grid, make all the settings whole-pixel numbers.

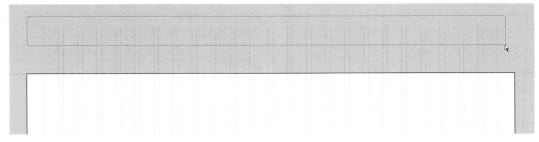

4.16 Select the top anchor points of the grid with the Direct Selection tool.

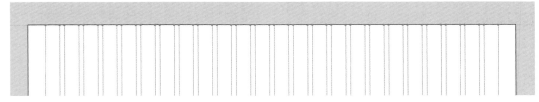

4.17 Move the anchor points to the edge of the artboard.

Making the Gridlines Fit

Now you have a nice 24-column grid. The last thing to do at this point is resize the gridlines so they fit nicely on the artboard. It's an optional step, but it helps when you have multiple artboards so you don't have grids overlap other artboards. To make them fit, follow these steps:

1. With the Direct Selection tool ![cursor icon] (A), drag to select all the anchor points on the top of the grid (**4.16**).

2. Use the arrow keys to nudge the anchor points until they sit at the top of the artboard (**4.17**).

3. Repeat for the bottom side so that all the vertical grid lines fit within the bounds of the artboard.

4. With the Direct Selection tool (A), select the two horizontal gridlines by clicking on their respective line segments. Press Delete twice to remove these two horizontal lines, as you do not really need them.

5. Press ⌘S/Ctrl+S to save your work.

NOTE When you select a line segment with the Direct Selection tool, the segment is selected, but the anchor points on each end are not. Pressing Delete removes only the segment; pressing Delete again removes the anchor points.

Applying the Grid to Multiple Artboards

You started with one artboard; as you begin to design more of the application, you may need to create multiple artboards in this single document. This 24-column grid is versatile enough to be useful on every page of the app. The question remains: How can you get this grid on every artboard in the document without having to copy and paste to each, or worse, recreate the previous steps on each artboard? The answer is stunningly simple.

1. Click the New Artboard button ⬚ at the bottom of the Artboard panel three times to add three more artboards to the document.

2. Select the grid with the Selection tool ▸ (V).

3. Choose Edit > Cut (⌘X/Ctrl+X) to cut the grid to the clipboard.

4. Choose Edit > Paste on All Artboards (⌘⌥⇧V/ Ctrl+Alt+Shift+V) .

   This brilliant shortcut pastes the grid to every artboard in exactly the same spot as where it was cut.

To add some variety to the layout, create a different grid for the landing page than you would on the rest of the application. All you would need to do is delete a grid from one of the artboards and follow the steps to create a new grid with different properties. When it comes to grids, Illustrator allows precision, speed, and flexibility. By using these tools, you'll find it easier to create and maintain grids than ever before.

Achieving Pixel Precision

I used to be a diehard Photoshop user. But I became frustrated with how difficult creating and maintaining large projects was with it and wanted a more efficient tool for my web design projects. I had tried several times over the last ten years to use Illustrator for web and UI design, only to be stopped in my tracks by the one thing that killed it—the lack of pixel-precise drawing features. My designs suffered from unwanted anti-aliasing (heretofore referred to as "fuzzy-edge syndrome") and a general lack of character that Photoshop made easy. Chances are you fit in this same camp; that may be the reason you're reading this book right now.

I made the switch for good when Adobe rolled out Illustrator CS4 in 2008. It turned out that Illustrator already included a few features for enabling pixel precision, I just didn't know those features were available or how to use them. Once I got it figured out, it was easy to walk away from Photoshop (for UI design, at least) for good. With CS5 and CS6, Adobe has made creating pixel-precise designs even easier (**4.18**).

4.18 The left side of the button suffers from fuzzy-edge syndrome. The right side is crisp thanks to the pixel-snapping features in Illustrator CS5 and later.

Pixel Preview Mode

The first feature Illustrator provides for ensuring pixel-precise artwork is Pixel Preview mode (⌘⌥Y/Ctrl+Alt+Y). The default Preview mode in Illustrator allows you to view your artwork as it would print. Objects are smooth and crisp no matter how far you zoom into your design. This mode is perfect for creating illustrations, logos, typography, or other illustrative elements that don't need to be pixel-precise.

However, when creating UI elements like buttons, widgets, or rules, using Preview mode paints an unrealistic picture of how these objects appear on the web or mobile devices, with the exception of newer ultra-high resolution devices. Using Pixel Preview mode renders your design on the screen at 72 pixels per inch, just like a raster-based application such as Photoshop would. When you zoom in, you can see how your objects and effects look on a bitmap display (**4.19**). This is referred to as anti-aliasing. The application inserts extra pixels of related colors to simulate a smooth curve.

Pixel Preview mode is great as a diagnostic tool, perfect for visualizing how your artwork will render on the low-resolution displays that are still fairly common today. It's great for viewing how Photoshop and Illustrator effects (to be discussed in Chapter 6) render on the screen. If you are a Photoshop user, you can also use it as your full-time view mode to provide some comfort and familiarity as you try to switch.

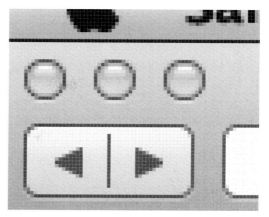

4.19 Pixel Preview mode allows you to see vectors as if they were bitmaps.

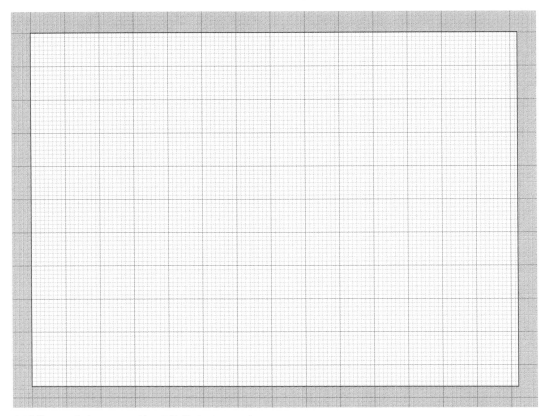

4.20 Illustrator's document-wide grid is like having graph paper on your screen.

Aligning Objects to the Pixel Grid

In Illustrator's application preferences (⌘K/ Ctrl+K), you can specify and view a customizable document-wide grid that is akin to graph paper (**4.20**). This is separate from the guide-based grid you created in the last section. However, in my opinion, this extremely loose yet very restrictive grid structure is really only useful for technical drawings. It's also inefficient, because it can be visually intrusive and has to be toggled on and off manually.

Since the end product of UI design is viewed on a pixel-based screen, it makes sense that it should be designed to match a pixel-based grid. Illustrator's answer for that need is the pixel grid. This grid is separate from both the document-wide grid and the guide-based grid. It's made up of one-pixel increments and allows for extremely precise drawing. In Pixel Preview mode (⌘⌥Y/Ctrl+Alt+Y), this grid is viewable when you zoom in to 600% or closer (**4.21**).

One of the newest features to take advantage of this grid is the ability to seamlessly and automatically align objects to the pixel grid as you draw. It enables you to keep your objects from having fuzzy edges in Pixel Preview mode by snapping the dimensions to whole-pixel values. Fuzzy-edge syndrome occurs when an object is either sized at sub-pixel increments (for example, a width of 400.3456 px) or sits on a sub-pixel X or Y point. Since Illustrator is a vector-based program, you have the ability to size and place artwork anywhere on the screen with up to 3-decimal-point precision, which can be helpful when creating print documents.

Since displays use pixels to render artwork, placing an object off of the pixel grid will cause it to blur; the screen can't color half of a pixel, so it anti-aliases it in order to keep pixel from looking jagged, which is where the fuzzy edge comes in. Keeping your objects on the pixel grid by having whole numbers in the object dimensions ensures that your artwork will render without fuzzy edges, appearing exactly the way you'd expect it. It's especially helpful when dealing with strokes.

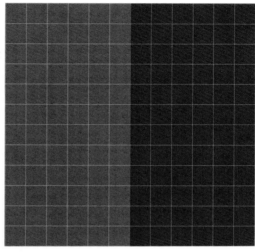

4.21 The pixel grid (which is filled in to show pixel detail) is displayed when in Pixel Preview mode and zoomed in closer than 600%.

You can enable or disable pixel alignment in a three ways:

- You can set pixel alignment on or off in the advanced section of the New Document dialog box when creating a new document (**4.22**).

- If you didn't turn the setting on when you created a new document, you can do so at any time from the Transform panel menu (**4.23**).

- You can control pixel alignment on an object-specific basis by toggling the option in the Transform panel's options pane (**4.24**). You can view these extra options by choosing Show Options from the Transform panel menu.

Since pixel alignment is a fairly new feature, opinions vary on whether you should let Illustrator control pixel-precise placement or whether you should turn the feature off and manage it yourself. I feel that as you begin to design UIs with Illustrator, you'll find the method that works best for you.

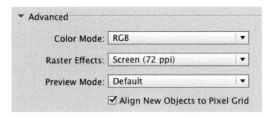

4.22 The Align New Objects to Pixel Grid setting in the New Document dialog box

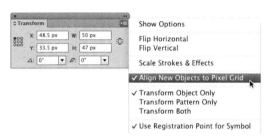

4.23 Turning on pixel alignment in the Transform panel menu

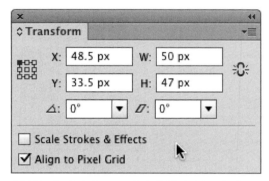

4.24 Toggle pixel alignment for individual objects in the Transform panel options pane.

4.25 The Control panel Transform fields

Coordinates and Reference Points

The Transform panel can also be a great tool to aid in achieving pixel-precise artwork. The Transform panel contains four fields: two for positioning elements according to values on the X and Y axis, and two for setting the width and height of an object. It also has the reference point locator, which is used for setting the point on an object that will act as the anchor for transformations (like rotations or scaling). You'll also find these fields in the Control panel when an object is selected (**4.25**).

It's really easy to use coordinates to precisely place your artwork anywhere on the artboard. This is a perfect opportunity to begin working on the Wheelr mockup. The first thing you need to do is add the simulated browser chrome. This has been created as a separate file that can be linked in this document via the Place command:

1. Using the document created earlier in the chapter, select Artboard 1 in the artboard navigator. This will place the artboard in the view and make it active.

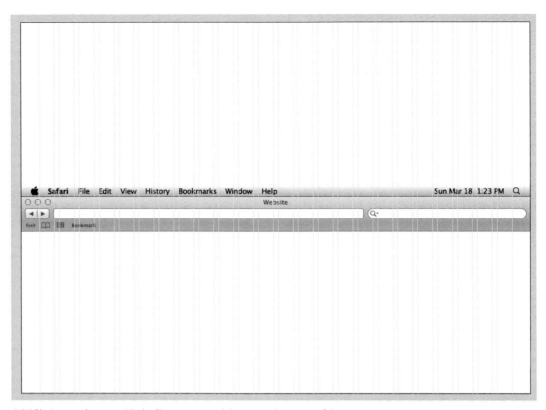

4.26 Placing an element with the Place command drops it in the center of the view.

2. Download the simulated browser chrome file at: www.peachpit.com/UIwithAI/ch4/ browser-chrome.ai. Once you've down-loaded the file to your computer, choose File > Place.

When you import an element using the Place command, it's dropped in the center of the current view based on its origin point (**4.26**). Since the object needs to be at the top of Artboard 1, using the X and Y value inputs in the Control panel will be the most precise way to get the object in place. The reference point locator in the Control panel shows the current origin point to be the center of the object.

3. Select the object and click the top left square on the reference point locator to change the object's point of origin (**4.27**).

   The X and Y values in the Control panel will change to reflect the new reference point. This doesn't affect the placement of an object; rather, it shows the location of that particular point.

4. Type *0* into the X and Y input fields in the Control panel.

   Because the placed object's reference point was the top-left corner, using zero for the x and y fields moves that point in the top-left corner of the artboard.

4.27 Change the origin point of an object with the reference point locator.

The Mathematician Within

The X, Y, W, and H input fields in the Transform panel and Control panel are much smarter than they initially appear. First, they will allow you to specify a particular unit of measure without changing the ruler units. For example, if you were working with pixels and wanted to make an object two inches wide, you would perform the following step:

1. Type *2 in* in the W (width) field and press Enter/Return. Illustrator resizes the object and automatically converts the units to pixels.

   Second, you can use the Transform inputs to do math.

2. To make an object 150 percent larger, add *150%* or *1.5* after the existing number (**4.28**) in the field and press Enter/Return. You can add, subtract, and divide using the same method.

If you want to resize an object proportionally, hold down the ⌘/Ctrl key as you press Enter/Return. Illustrator will adjust the width or height in proportion to what you entered.

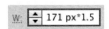

4.28 You can use the Transform inputs to perform math equations.

Beginning the Layout

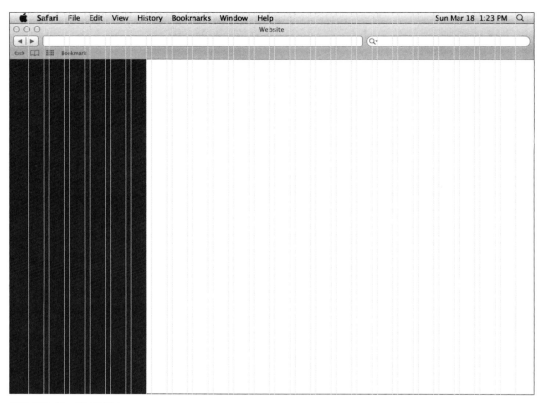

4.29 First, draw the sidebar.

Now that you have a grid and the browser chrome in place, you can start putting together the design of the screen. In this chapter, you'll begin by putting in the main structural divisions for the UI as well as the basic typography.

First, you'll create the sidebar area. This will hold the logo, main navigation, and social features for the app:

1. Draw a rectangle on the left side of the artboard. If the object has a stroke, remove it and set the fill to #2d2d2d.

2. With the rectangle selected, use the width and height fields in the Control panel to make the rectangle 267 px wide and 674 px tall. Place it at the far left of the artboard and under the browser chrome (**4.29**).

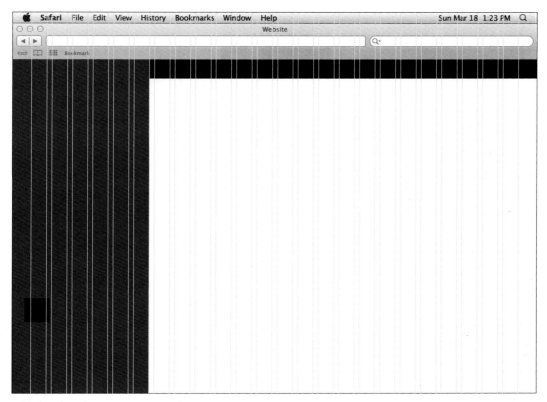

4.30 Then draw the section navigation bar.

3. Within the sidebar, draw a 49 px wide by 49 px tall square and give it a black fill and no stroke. This will act as the thumbnail image for a Suggested Friends feature.

4. Draw another rectangle that starts under the chrome and just to the right of the sidebar. It should be 38 pixels tall and the width of the remaining area. Set the fill of this rectangle #000000 (**4.30**). This will be the section navigation bar.

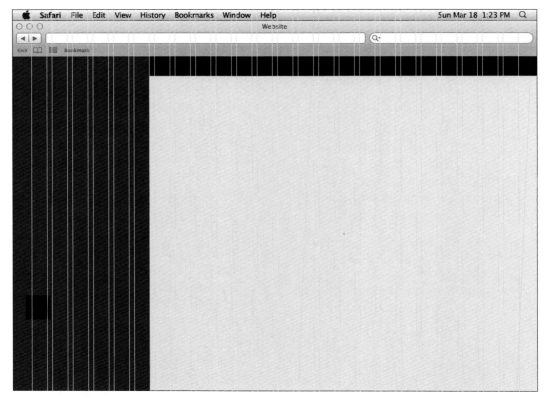

4.31 Finish up by drawing the content area background.

5. Draw a rectangle that fills the remaining space in the artboard. Give it it a color of #e6e6e6 (**4.31**). This will be the main content area.

6. Press ⌘S/Ctrl+S to save your work.

Lining Up Strokes

Filled objects are easy to line up on the grid, but objects with strokes pose a problem. When using strokes on objects, Illustrator places the stroke across the line segment. This means that a one-pixel stroke will cover half a pixel on each side of the line segment. Using pixel alignment on the object will prevent the stroke from looking fuzzy in Pixel Preview mode, but the fact that the stroke is placed over the line segment isn't accurate to how the object will render in a browser.

In HTML/CSS, the browser box model renders all borders on the outside of the object. To stay true to this rendering, you'll want to have your strokes in Illustrator do the same thing so that you have accurate measurements for development. To demonstrate how to do this, you'll create the picture frame for the car photos in the mockup.

1. Draw a 142 px x 142 px rectangle in the content area of the mockup and give it a white fill and a 4 px black stroke.

    If you zoom in, you'll notice how the line segment sits smack dab in the middle of the stroke (**4.32**).

2. Select the rectangle and click the Stroke link in the Control panel (**4.33**).

4.32 Strokes are centered over line segments by default.

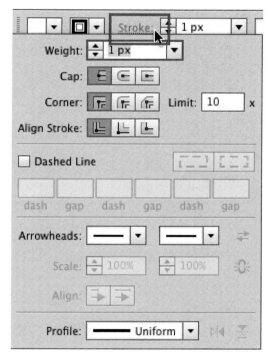

4.33 Click the link in the Control panel to conveniently access the Stroke panel.

3. Click Align Stroke to Outside (**4.34**).

   Now the rectangle looks the way it's supposed to, with the stroke outside the object (**4.35**).

Things work a little differently with open objects and rules. Aligning a stroke to the inside or outside is not enabled for these objects. Because you have pixel alignment enabled, the stroke will automatically move tho the nearest pixel to keep from getting fuzzy-stroke syndrome:

1. Select the Line Segment tool 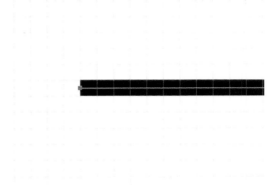 (\) and draw a 223 pixel-wide horizontal rule in the sidebar. Remove the fill and give it a 1 px stroke, with the color set to #1d1d1d.

   This stroke will be used as a dividing line between sections in the sidebar.

2. Turn on Pixel Preview mode by selecting View Pixel Preview (⌘⌥Y/Ctrl+Alt+Y).

3. Zoom in to view how the stroke automatically adjusts to stay on the pixel grid (**4.36**).

4. Press ⌘S/Ctrl+S to save your work.

NOTE For more information on the browser box model, go to http://d.pr/wdCS.

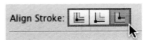

4.34 The Align Stroke to Outside button

4.35 The stroke aligned to the outside of the segment

4.36 Pixel alignment automatically adjusts strokes to fit on the pixel grid. (The background color has been hidden so that you can more easily see what's happening.)

Typography for the UI

With the main structure created, it's time to move on to typography. Good typography in a UI can emphasize and give clarity to app structure and hierarchy. In some applications, it can actually be the interface itself. If you have experience in setting type for print documents, there are some factors you need to consider when you're setting type for a UI.

Looking Good on the Screen

First, you'll need to think about font choices. You can use web fonts from sources like FontSquirrel (http://www.fontsquirrel.com) or the standard fonts that come with every Mac or Windows system. For system fonts, there is some parity between the two. Choosing a font that both systems have will ensure a similar experience no matter the platform. Make sure to use the same font in your mockup that you are going to use in the final UI.

The next thing to consider is how your type will render on the screen. One of the big pushes in the UI design world is for a tool that will render type the same way as it does in the browser. While I think that is a great idea, it's difficult for me to imagine it happening anytime soon, simply because of all the variables that go into displaying type on a screen. You have the browser or app rendering engine, screen resolution, computer platform, and quality of typeface working against this idea. In the meantime, my philosophy is to get as close as I can in Illustrator and let the screen do what the screen will do.

That said, Illustrator recently inherited a feature from Photoshop that makes type rendering even better. You can now set the anti-aliasing method of the typeface you're using to get better results for type destined for the web or mobile devices. There are subtle differences in the way each method affects your type. **4.37** shows a comparison of the four modes on Helvetica Neue.

You'll see how it works in the real world by adding a current section headline to the navigation bar in the mockup. To make things easier to see for now, go ahead and hide your guides by choosing View > Guides > Hide Guides (⌘;/Ctrl+;).

1. Select the Type tool T̲ (T) and set some point type by clicking once in the navigation bar. Type *The Latest* as the name of this section. Press Escape to leave type-editing mode.

    Illustrator defaults new text to Myriad Pro, which always seems to render well. However, since I don't have a web font license for Myriad and not everyone using the app will likely have it installed on his or her system, you'll change it to something else.

Antialiasing None

Antialiasing Sharp

Antialiasing Crisp

Antialiasing Strong

4.37 Anti-aliasing modes

2. With the Selection tool (V), click once on the text to select it and then click the Character link in the Control panel. This will reveal the Character panel.

3. Choose Helvetica Neue Bold from the font list. If you don't have Helvetica, choose Arial Bold instead.

4. Change the size to 18 px and give it a white fill by clicking the white swatch in the Swatches panel.

   These typefaces really highlight the wonky rendering effects of the Sharp anti-aliasing mode (**4.38**).

   At the bottom right of the Character panel is a drop-down menu of anti-aliasing options (**4.39**).

5. Choose the Crisp setting from the drop-down menu.

   The Sharp setting is the default, and I have found after a lot of experimentation and comparison that the Crisp setting will give you the best results the majority of the time.

4.38 The section headline looks odd when using Sharp anti-aliasing.

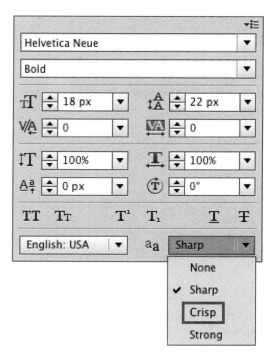

4.39 Accessing the anti-aliasing modes from the Character panel

| **The Latest** | Your Crew | You | Everybody |

4.40 The completed section navigation bar with horizontal navigation

Typesetting Basics

Now that you have type rendering looking good, you'll get the rest of the type into the mockup. You will use a mixture of point type and area type so you can get the feel for how and when to use each.

Using Point Type

Start by finishing off the section navigation bar:

1. Select the Type tool (T) and click once in the navigation bar you created earlier to set a point type object. Type *Your Crew* as one of the navigation items.

2. When you're finished, press Escape. This is the fastest way to exit text-editing mode.

3. Finish off the navigation by typing *You* and *Everybody* with point type.

4. Select all three blocks of type and use the Character panel to make them Helvetica Neue Bold (or Arial Bold) at 12 px. Give them a white fill.

5. Move the type into place so that it matches the type in **4.40**. You don't need to be precise at this point since you are still in the rough stage of the layout. Things could change as you move on.

   Now complete the text for the sidebar.

TIP Using point type as opposed to area type for horizontal navigation elements gives you much more flexibility in moving, aligning, and spacing the individual blocks of type.

6. For the main app navigation, click once with the Type tool and type *Collection*, *Crew*, and *Profile*. Use a hard return after each word with the Return key so that each word is on its own line (**4.41**).

7. With the area text still selected, select the Eyedropper tool (I) and click the section headline text, *The Latest*.

   Not only does this trick make styling your text fast and easy, but it also ensures consistency in the UI. Just like you don't want to use too many different fonts in a document, using too many different sizes and styles can make a layout look cluttered and inconsistent.

TIP For vertical navigation elements, it's easier to keep all the text in one block as opposed to separate ones. You can use leading and paragraph spacing to manage the distances between elements here in a way that is easy to replicate in HTML.

Using Area Type

For the Activity section of the sidebar, we will stray away from point type and use area type instead. The text in this section may end up being lengthy, so we want the line wraps to happen automatically like in the browser.

1. To set a block of area type, select the Type tool (T), and then click and drag a rectangle in the sidebar (**4.42**).

2. Type the lines from **4.43** in the text box, using a hard return between each line.

4.41 The sidebar with vertical navigation

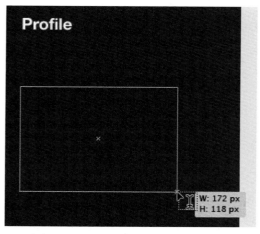

4.42 Click and drag with the Type tool to create an area type container.

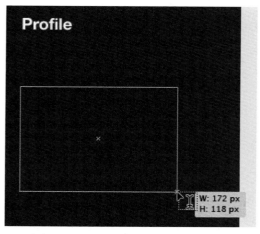

4.43 The Recent Activity feature in the sidebar

3. Style this text using Helvetica Neue (or Arial) at 12 px. Give it a white fill if it doesn't already have one. Press Escape to exit text-editing mode.

   Using area type allows you to constrain the width of a type container automatically. But how do you resize a container once it's set? There are two ways to accomplish this:

   • To manually adjust the width or height, use the Direct Selection tool (A). This will allow you to select a single segment of the container and then either drag it or use the arrow keys to resize it.

   • If you know precisely what size you'd like the container to be, select the text and choose Area Type Options from the Type menu. In the dialog box that appears, you can input exact numbers for height and width.

4. To simulate the link in the activity text, double-click the type container with the Selection tool (V). This is another handy way to edit text without having to click the Type tool first.

5. Click and drag over the first couple of words to select them (**4.44**).

6. In the Character panel, click the Underline button (**4.45**).

4.44 Underlining text to indicate a link

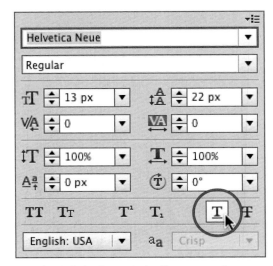

4.45 The Underline button in the Character panel

Adding the Final Headline

You're almost done with the first iteration. Now you'll add the final headline for a Suggested Friends feature in the sidebar and a label for the picture frame in the content area (**4.46**).

1. Click with the Type tool (T) just above the small black square in the sidebar. Type *Popular Collectors*.

2. Style this text with the Eyedropper tool (I) by clicking the text that reads "The Latest."

3. Use point type to create a label called *Image Title* for the picture frame box in the content area.

4. Style this text with Helvetica Neue Bold (or Arial Bold) at 12 px.

5. With the text still selected, choose the Eyedropper tool and click the section navigation rectangle.

   You used the Eyedropper tool before to pull the color and type attributes from another text element. You can also color your text by pulling the color from a shape. Again, this helps keep consistency in the interface.

6. Press ⌘S/Ctrl+S to save your work.

TIP You can use the Eyedropper tool to pull the color from any object. To pull a color from a portion of a gradient or a placed bitmap image, hold the Shift key while you click the color you want to sample.

4.46 Create the section headline for the suggested friends feature.

Creating Character Styles

You'll need to take care of one final detail before you move on. Creating character styles now will help out immensely as you add more text to the mockup. Character styles save text-formatting information in a way that it can be applied to other text elements with a click.

To create a character style:

1. Select the text to use as the basis for the style. For this example, choose the section navigation headline, "The Latest."

2. Open the Character Styles panel either from the panel groups onscreen or by choosing Window > Type > Character Styles.

3. Click the Create New Style button (**4.47**).

   The new style appears in the panel list with the name "Character Style 1." Rename it so it's easier to figure out later when you need to use it.

4. Double-click the style in the list and rename it *H1*. Press Enter.

   That was easy! If you need to edit the formatting options of the style, choose Character Style Options from the panel menu. In the dialog box that appears, you can edit pretty much any formatting attribute you need (**4.48**).

5. Create character styles for the other text elements as you see fit.

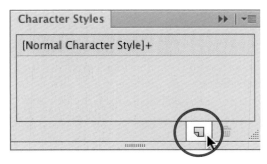

4.47 Creating a new character style

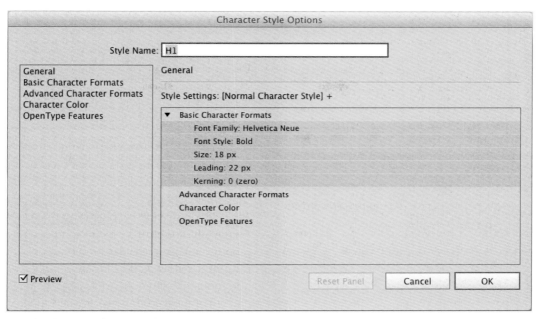

4.48 The Character Style Options dialog box

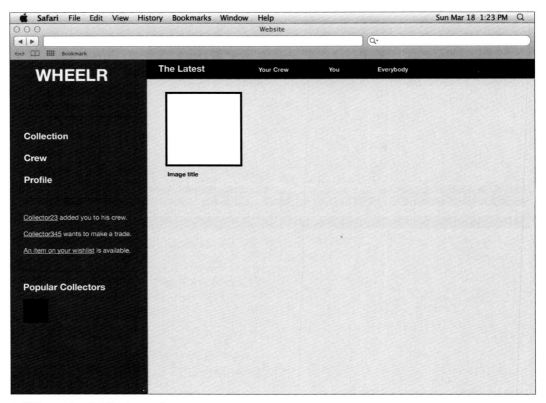

4.49 The mockup for Wheelr … so far

Conclusion

Go ahead and place the last few elements to match **4.49**. It may not look like much right now, but don't be discouraged. Creating a good user experience happens best in layers. It's vital to make sure that you have the right content and have thought through the interactions before you start thinking about style. Once you have those things figured out, you can move on to creating and polishing the UI.

You began with a wireframe by creating the basic shapes and setting the type. In the next chapter, you'll learn how to use graphic styles and symbols to speed up UI element creation. You'll also learn how to take advantage of layers to organize your artwork.

TABLE 4.1 Keyboard Shortcuts in This Chapter

	MAC	PC
Show/Hide Rulers	⌘R	Ctrl+R
Undo	⌘Z	Ctrl+Z
Hide/Show Guides	⌘; (semicolon)	Ctrl+; (semicolon)
Lock/Unlock Guides	⌘⌥; (semicolon)	Ctrl+Alt+; (semicolon)
Make Guides	⌘5	Ctrl+5
Release Guides	⌘⌥5	Ctrl+Alt+5
Copy	⌘C	Ctrl+C
Align Panel	⇧F7	Shift+F7
Show/Hide Smart Guides	⌘U	Ctrl+U
Save	⌘S	Ctrl+S
Cut	⌘X	Ctrl+X
Paste in Place	⌘⇧V	Ctrl+Shift+V
Paste on All Artboards	⌘⇧⌥V	Ctrl+Shift+Alt+V
Pixel Preview Mode	⌘⌥Y	Ctrl+Alt+Y
Preferences	⌘K	Ctrl+K

WHEELR

🔍

COLLECTION

CREW

PROFILE

Collector23 added you to his crew.

Collector345 wants to make a trade.

THE LATEST   Your Crew

Image Title

5

GETTING STYLISH WITH GRAPHICS

Chapter Overview

In the last chapter, you began the creation of a user interface design for Wheelr. You created a grid, added basic elements to define UI structure, and set some type. In this chapter, you'll harness the power of Illustrator's vector-based features and effects to turbocharge your design workflow. Illustrator provides three tools to assist in creating and reusing your beautiful UI elements:

- The Appearance panel
- Graphic styles
- Symbols

You'll use these tools to enhance the mockup for Wheelr. You'll also learn how to use the Layers panel to organize your artwork as you tighten up the layout. By the way, if you've been following along and creating the UI design, now would be a great time to save your work.

Adding Style to Appearances

Executing a design that I have in my head or on paper has always been a fun challenge to tackle. I absolutely love that part of my job. When the tool I use makes getting that vision onto the screen easy, it's a glorious thing. That being said, I think the addition of the Appearance panel and graphic styles are two of the best things to happen to Illustrator since its inception. The Appearance panel allows for a lot of flexibility in the creation of a design element, and graphic styles make it simple to apply that design to any other object on the page. Let's take a look at how these work together.

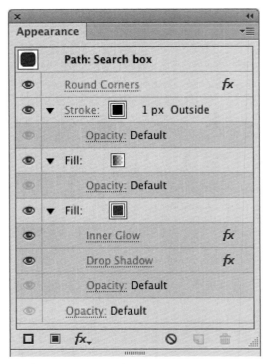

5.1 The Appearance panel

Using the Appearance Panel

In Illustrator, the appearance of an object can be thought of as a stack of attributes viewed from the top down. The Appearance panel (accessed using the keyboard shortcut Shift-F6) is the tool you use to manage this stack. It gives appearance information about all the attributes of an object on the screen. You can view the object's fill, stroke, opacity, and any effects that have been applied (**5.1**). At first glance, the panel may seem like only a tool for viewing information about a selected object, but it provides real power for creating screen graphics. To show you just how powerful it is, let's use it to create a common UI element.

Creating a Search Box

Sites and applications that deal with a lot of content (both native and user-generated) typically use a search box as the mechanism for finding that content. The web has many examples of this design pattern from which you can draw inspiration for your UI designs (**5.2**). Since there are many ways to style one with HTML and CSS, you'll want to specify the look that your developers should match when the system is built.

The next set of steps describes how to create a search box (**5.3**) that will reside in the sidebar of the Wheelr mockup. This search box will need a dark background, as well as an inner shadow and a drop shadow to give it some depth on the page.

1. Draw a 221 px x 28 px rectangle and place it at the top of the sidebar, underneath the Wheelr name.

2. In the Appearance panel, select the Fill layer (**5.4**).

3. Give the rectangle a fill by double-clicking the Fill button in the Tools panel (**5.5**).

   Using the Color Picker, you can quickly add a fill to an object. It allows you to choose a color by clicking in a color field or spectrum, entering numbers in one of the color models, or choosing a color swatch.

NOTE If the grid you created in the last chapter is visible, hide it by choosing View > Guides > Hide Guides (⌘⌥; [semicolon]/Ctrl+Option+; [semicolon]), which makes it easier to see what you are doing.

5.2 Real-world search box examples

5.3 This is the search box design you'll create.

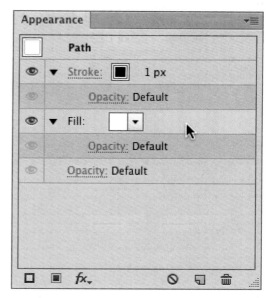

5.4 Selecting a Fill layer

5.5 Double-clicking the Fill button opens the Color Picker.

4. Enter *4d4d4d* in the hexadecimal color value field (**5.6**), and then click OK.

5. In the Appearance panel, select the Stroke layer. This time, double-click the Stroke button in the Tools panel and assign a hexadecimal color of *1d1d1d*.

6. In the Stroke panel, click the Align Stroke to Outside button ⌊⌐⌋.

7. Press ⌘S/Crtl+S to save your work.

5.7 shows what you have so far. You need to do a couple more things before it really looks like a search box, though.

NOTE Adding a stroke to an object automatically gives it a 1 px stroke that is aligned to center of the line segment. Align this stroke to the outside of the object so it matches the browser's box model.

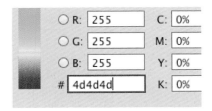

5.6 The hexadecimal color field allows you to specify web colors as you would in CSS.

5.7 This search box is still pretty boring.

Color Options

There are several ways to add color to a fill or stroke of an object. Besides using the Color Picker as described in the creation of the search box, you can also add color in the following ways:

- Clicking a swatch in the Swatches panel

- Using the Color panel to mix colors

In the Appearance panel and Control panel, clicking the Fill and Stroke pop-ups ▣ ▾ □ ▾ opens the Swatches panel; pressing the Shift key and clicking will show the Color panel.

Having options is great because you can find a way that works best for you, rather than being forced to work how the application thinks you should.

Stacking Appearance Attributes

The awesome thing about the Appearance panel is the ability to "stack" strokes, fills, and effects on a single object. Even better, each stroke and fill can have independent effects, opacity, and transformations. Let's dive a little deeper with this idea.

Adding Rounded Corners

To start, this search box needs some rounded corners. Besides looking more approachable, rounding the corners keeps them from acting like four arrows that lead the eye out of the object.

1. Select the search box rectangle and then click the Path layer at the top of the Appearance panel (**5.8**).

2. Choose Effect > Stylize > Round Corners.

3. In the resulting dialog box, make the corners 14 px and click OK to see the result (**5.9**).

TIP To create the perfect lozenge-shaped box, make the rounded corners as close to half the height of the object as possible. This keeps the corners from looking like the edges of a bullet.

NOTE Illustrator has a tool for drawing rectangles with rounded corners, but it leaves you with a very inflexible object. Once the object is drawn, the corners are locked in at that radius. You would have to select individual points to edit the shape to keep from distorting the corners, or redraw it if you wanted a different radius.

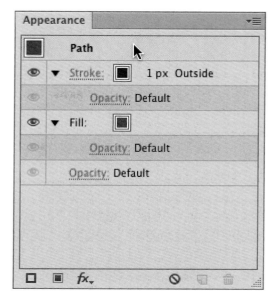

5.8 Selecting the Path layer ensures that an effect is applied to all attribute layers automatically.

5.9 The typical search box shape

Note that in the previous steps you applied the rounded-corner effect to the Path layer rather than the fill or stroke layer. Doing this ensures that both stroke and fill receive the effect. That way, you don't have to add the effect to each appearance layer independently.

The other thing that is great about the rounded-corner effect (and all others like it) is that it is a "live" effect. So as you resize the object, the corners don't distort. In this case, that also means the corners will always have a 14 px radius no matter how you resize the object. You can also change the radius or remove the effect altogether at any time without affecting the underlying object.

You'll enhance this rectangle by adding an inner shadow and a drop shadow to create an inset look.

Creating an Inner Shadow Effect

Many search boxes use an effect called an inner shadow. It makes the text field look like it is set into the page, adding depth and interest to the design. Illustrator doesn't have a built-in inner shadow effect yet, so you'll need to create an equivalent:

1. Select the search box and then click the Fill layer in the Appearance panel.

2. Choose Effect > Stylize > Inner Glow. In the Inner Glow dialog box, set the mode to Normal, and then click the swatch to the right of the Mode pop-up (**5.10**). Enter *000000* in the Color Picker's hexadecimal color field.

3. Set Opacity to 65% and Blur to 4 px, and click OK to see the result (**5.11**).

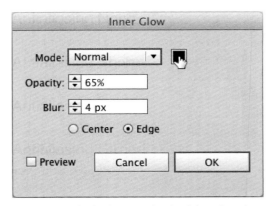

5.10 Set the color for the inner glow by clicking the color swatch icon.

5.11 The shadow is beginning to take shape.

4. With the search box still selected, click the Add New Fill ■ button at the bottom of the Appearance panel.

   This will add another fill to the object using the same color as the previous one. This fill will be used to add a one-color gradient that is transparent at one end so the top of the inner glow peeks through.

5. Give this new fill a gradient by pressing the > key.

6. In the Gradient panel, double-click the white color stop to open the Color panel (**5.12**).

7. Choose Web Safe RGB from the panel menu and set the color to *4d4d4d*.

8. Double-click the black color stop and repeat step 7. Set the Opacity to 0%.

9. Type *90* in the Gradient panel's Angle field △. Press Enter to view the result (**5.13**).

NOTE If you haven't created any gradients yet, the object will be filled with a default black-to-white gradient. If you don't have that default gradient, press the ⌘/Ctrl key and click the gradient swatch ▨ · in the Gradient panel (accessed by choosing Window > Gradient) to reset the default gradient. Resetting it will make this series of steps easier to follow.

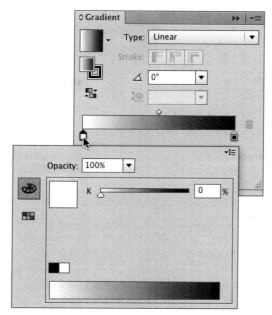

5.12 Double-clicking a color stop will allow you to add color to the gradient.

5.13 The completed inner shadow effect

Adding a Drop Shadow

With the inner shadow complete, you're ready to add the drop shadow. This drop shadow will use a white fill with a very low opacity level. The 2 px Y-offset reveals the drop shadow by nudging it down from the stroke.

5.14 The final inset effect for the search box

1. Make sure the search box is still selected. In the Appearance panel, select the bottom Fill layer and then choose Effect > Stylize > Drop Shadow.

2. Set the Opacity to 15%, the X-offset to 0, and the Y-offset to 2 px.

3. Click the color swatch at the bottom of the dialog box and enter *ffffff* in the hexadecimal color field. Click OK to see the result (**5.14**).

4. Press ⌘S/Ctrl+S to save your work.

This inner shadow technique is very customizable. The trick when creating the effect is to make sure that the fill that creates the search field's background and both colors of the gradient fill are the same color. These same steps would work the same no matter what color you use (**5.15**). You can finesse the inner glow's blur and opacity levels until it looks right to your eye.

All that's left to add to complete the search box is a magnifying glass icon. You'll add that later in the chapter.

TIP When creating effects like this, think about how they might be built with CSS. For example, the stroke that creates the border of the search box is aligned to the outside so that it mimics the box model. You used Normal since blending modes aren't yet supported in CSS.

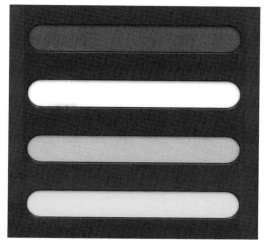

5.15 Changing the color of the search field

Objectivity

The great thing about this search box is that you can do the following things to it:

- Recolor it
- Change the corner radius
- Adjust the inner shadow and the drop shadow attributes
- Add other effects easily from the Appearance panel

Selecting and moving the box around on the screen is a snap, too, because it's still just one simple rectangle.

Each effect is self-contained on the object, so you don't have to worry about selecting all the different elements before moving or transforming it. You can view it in Outline mode (View > Outline or ⌘Y/Ctrl+Y) to see what I mean.

Creating the Photo Frame

Another popular design pattern on the web and in apps is a photo frame. These frames are usually made to look like pictures with slightly curled edges, creating a small shadow underneath (**5.16**). If you've been following along with the Wheelr mockup, you created the basis for this effect in the last chapter (**5.17**).

This square will eventually multiply to become a group of photos showing the latest cars added by users of the system. Since this content should be the focus of the page, you'll use the Appearance panel to give it some depth. This is accomplished by using the Arch effect to give it a curved drop shadow.

1. Select the 142 px wide by 142 px tall square. In the Appearance panel, hold the Shift key while clicking the Color pop-up to access the Color panel (**5.18**).

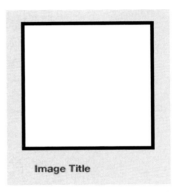

5.16 Photo frame effect as seen on www.mixel.cc

5.17 The starting point for Wheelr's photo frame

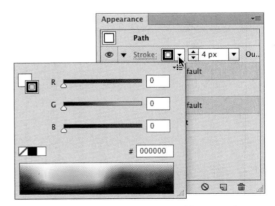

5.18 Shift-click the Color pop-up to quickly access the Color panel.

2. Change the stroke color *#ededed*.

   The stroke may be a little light right now
   (**5.19**), but this background will become
   darker in the next chapter.

3. In the Appearance panel, click the Add
   New Fill button ▣.

   This adds a new fill to the top of the appearance stack. You'll use this new fill as the
   basis for the photo frame's drop shadow.

4. Drag the new fill to the bottom of the
   stack (**5.20**) and set the color to *#000000*.

5. With the new fill selected, choose Effect >
   Warp > Arch. Set the Bend to 4% and
   click OK.

   At this point, you won't see the shadow.
   You'll add another effect to position
   it correctly.

6. Choose Effect > Distort & Transform > Transform. Set the Vertical setting to 7 px (**5.21**).

Image Title

5.19 The photo frame has a very light outline for now.

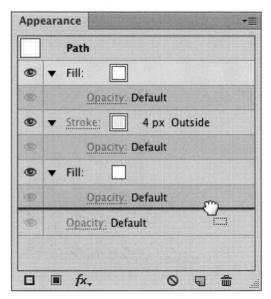

5.20 Dragging the topmost fill to the bottom to change
the stacking order

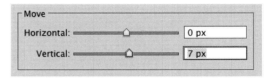

5.21 Moving an attribute layer with the Distort and Transform effect

7. Click the Opacity link of this Fill layer and change the opacity to 35% (**5.22**).

8. Press ⌘S/Ctrl+S to save your work.

This Transform effect positions the black rectangle lower to give a drop shadow effect. The Arch effect gives the impression of a slight curl to the photo to add a bit of realism (**5.23**). You'll enhance the photo frame and its shadow a bit more in the next chapter.

NOTE If you don't see the Opacity link for an Appearance layer, click the triangle on the left of the layer to expand its attributes.

TIP Each Appearance layer has its own Opacity setting separate from that of the entire object. It can get confusing at times, as these Opacity links often appear right next to each other in the panel. The easiest way to determine the Opacity setting for an Appearance layer is to look for the one that is indented (**5.24**).

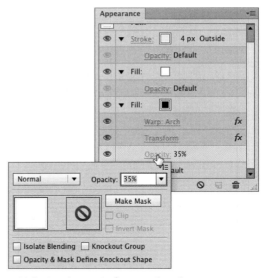

5.22 Setting the opacity for an attribute layer

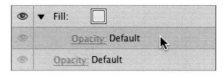

5.23 The start of the curled drop shadow effect

5.24 Appearance panel layer attributes are indicated by an indent and darker background.

Creating and Editing Graphic Styles

Creating the inner shadow and drop shadow effects on the search box and photo frame took a lot of steps. Thankfully, graphic styles enable you to add appearances to other objects without having to go through all the steps over and over again.

Graphic styles allow you to take a group of appearance attributes and effects and package them together in a reusable style. Once saved, the style can be applied an infinite number of times to any vector object on the screen (**5.25**). This helps increase efficiency when creating objects that need to look the same.

Creating a New Graphic Style

Creating a new graphic style is really easy:

1. Select the search box again. You'll use this object to set the style.

2. In the Graphic Styles panel (Shift-F5), click the New Graphic Style button 🔲 .

   This will create a new swatch in the panel with the name Graphic Style.

3. Double-click the new style and name it *Search Box*.

   Naming graphic styles is important. As you begin to create many of them in a project, distinguishing between them is easier when they have good, relevant names.

5.25 Using a graphic style allows you to make the top rectangle look like the bottom one with one click.

Editing the Style

Graphic styles also make updating your design more efficient. Imagine 10 other pages in this mockup that all had the search box on them. You decide the white drop shadow is a little too strong, so you want to decrease the opacity slightly. Here's how you can edit a graphic style to update all the other search boxes automatically:

1. Select the search box and click the Drop Shadow effect on the bottom Fill layer (**5.26**).

2. Change Opacity to 10% and click OK.

3. In the Appearance panel, choose Redefine Graphic Style "Search Box" from the panel menu (**5.27**).

   This action takes the change made to the graphic style and applies it to all other objects in the document that use it. Now go and take a break, because you just saved yourself a ton of time.

5.26 Clicking an effect link opens its dialog box for editing.

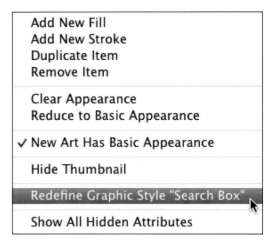

5.27 Redefining a graphic style after editing applies the change to all objects that have the style.

Using Symbols

A symbol is another Illustrator feature that helps create efficiency when dealing with objects that need to be repeated. If you've used Adobe Flash, the concept of a symbol will be familiar. Symbols were originally added to Illustrator to help with interoperability with Flash. Since CS5, however, they have gained features that benefit Illustrator-only use as well.

5.28 Drawing the magnifying glass handle

The main difference between a symbol and a graphic style is that a symbol is a self-contained art object rather than just a collection of appearance attributes. Symbols have their own layer structure and positioning information as well as advanced transformation and color capabilities. Let's take a look at how symbols can be used in the Wheelr mockup with the search box you just created in the previous section.

As mentioned earlier, the search box still needs a magnifying glass icon to distinguish it as such in the UI. Creating this icon is easy:

1. Inside the search box, draw a 10 px by 10 px circle with the Ellipse tool ⬭ (L).

2. Give it a 2 px stroke that is aligned to the inside and set *#2d2d2d* as the color.

3. With the Line Segment tool ╱ (\\), draw a handle for the icon. Hold the Shift key as you draw to constrain the segment to a 45-degree angle (**5.28**).

4. Give the handle a 2 px stroke and set *#2d2d2d* as the color.

5. Press ⌘S/Ctrl+S to save your work.

Creating a Symbol

Now that you have the icon in the search box (**5.29**), make the whole thing a symbol.

Creating a symbol is very straightforward:

1. Select the search box and the magnifying glass objects and press F8.

   The Symbol Options dialog box appears (**5.30**). Several important settings here determine the behavior of the new symbol.

2. Name the symbol *Search Box*.

3. Keep the Type setting at its default.

   The Type setting is important only if you plan to use this document in Flash. Movie clips in Flash have different uses than graphics. This setting has no effect on the object in Illustrator.

4. Set the registration point to the top left.

   The registration point determines the origin point of the symbol. The registration point is used when placing, resizing, or rotating a symbol. Where to place this registration point really is based on how you plan to use the symbol. I tend to place it in the top-left corner about 99% of the time.

5. Leave Enable Guides for 9-Slice Scaling deselected for now.

   Enabling this setting allows the symbol to be resized without distorting it. This feature is covered later on in the chapter.

5.29 The finished search box, ready to be made into a symbol

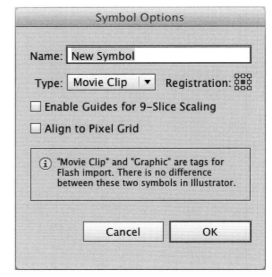

5.30 The Symbol Options dialog box

6. Select the Align to Pixel Grid option.

   For a symbol that uses effects and strokes in its appearance, turning this feature on helps to keep all the objects within it to stay on the pixel grid.

7. Click OK to create the symbol.

8. Press ⌘S/Ctrl+S to save your work.

TIP You can distinguish a symbol onscreen by the registration icon on the selection (**5.31**).

5.31 A symbol is indicated by the registration mark on the selection.

Working with Symbols

Once you have created a symbol, all the attributes that define it remain with the original contained in the Symbols panel. Any symbol on the artboard is considered an instance of the original symbol and any transformation made applies only to that instance.

Placing a Symbol Instance

You can place as many instances of a symbol as you need, and you can place them a couple of ways:

• **Drag an instance onto the artboard from the Symbols panel:** Using this method allows you to place an instance where you drop it on the artboard.

• **Click the Place Symbol Instance button ↳ at the bottom of the panel**: Using this method places the instance in the center of the view.

Editing a Symbol

You can transform a symbol instance with a tool like the Free Transform tool. To actually change the look of a symbol, you'll need to edit the symbol definition itself. Let's see how this works by changing the look of a duplicated symbol:

1. In the Symbols panel, select the Search Box symbol and choose Duplicate Symbol from the panel menu.

2. Click the Symbol Options button ▤ and rename the duplicated symbol *Search Box Active*. Select the Align to Pixel Grid option and click OK.

3. In the Symbols panel, double-click the symbol to enter isolation mode.

4. Select the object and click the bottom Fill layer in the Appearance panel.

5. Change the color of this fill to *#ffffff*.

Isolation Mode

Isolation mode is a useful feature for editing objects in groups as well as symbols. In this mode, other objects on the artboard are dimmed and cannot be selected or edited. By default, double-clicking a group or symbol on the artboard places it in isolation mode.

Once in isolation mode, any changes you make to an object happen in place. You can add or delete objects, or make transformations while in isolation. To exit isolation mode, simply press Escape.

6. Select the gradient Fill layer and change all color stops to white.

   The final symbol should look like **5.32**.

7. Press Escape to exit isolation mode.

8. Press ⌘S/Ctrl+S to save your work.

   With the white background completed, this symbol will act as the active search box in the mockup.

Swap Symbols

Illustrator can replace one symbol with another, which comes in handy for mocking up how the search box would change when a user clicks in it to enter search terms. To document this search interaction, you'll duplicate the current artboard and change the search box to the active state.

1. Duplicate the current artboard by choosing Duplicate Artboards from the Artboards panel menu. In the Artboards panel, drag up the new artboard so it's just underneath the old one (**5.33**).

2. Double-click the new artboard to make it active in the window.

   When you create the duplicate, Illustrator doesn't automatically bring it into the current view. If you don't perform this step, you could inadvertently edit the original artboard. I've done it a thousand times and it's a pain.

5.32 The alternate search box symbol

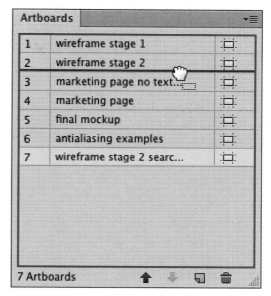

5.33 Dragging artboards into place

3. Select the search box on the new artboard. The Control panel has a pop-up panel labeled Replace; open the panel and click the Search Box Active symbol (**5.34**).

4. Press ⌘S/Ctrl+S to save your work.

   The search box on the artboard will now show the symbol with the white background. Clicking the Next and Previous buttons in the artboard navigator (found in the bottom-left corner of the document) will toggle between the two artboards, showing how the interaction works.

Resizing Symbols with 9-Slice Scaling

Symbols have one more amazing feature that makes life easier for a UI designer. Some elements in a UI may vary in size, like a text field or a background element; when using symbols for these objects, you can use 9-slice scaling to keep distortions from happening when you resize.

First, let's see what happens when you resize a symbol that doesn't have this setting enabled:

1. Select the search box that has the dark background.

2. Select the Free Transform tool (E) and drag the right edge handle of the symbol to resize it.

   Without 9-slice scaling enabled, the symbol looks like it ran into a wall. That's not the effect we are hoping to achieve (**5.35**).

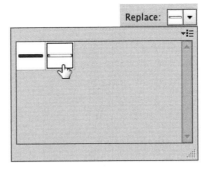

5.34 Swapping one symbol for another

5.35 Symbols get squished without 9-slice scaling enabled.

3. With the symbol selected, click the Reset button in the Control panel.

This button allows you to remove all transformations made to a symbol and returns it to its original state.

You can enable 9-slice scaling for a symbol at any time. Turn it on now and see how it affects the search box symbol.

4. In the Symbols panel, select the Search Box symbol and then click the Symbol Options button ▣.

5. Select the Enable Guides for 9-Slice Scaling option (**5.36**) and click OK.

6. Back on the artboard, double-click the search box to enter isolation mode.

When you double-click a symbol on the artboard, you'll see a dialog box letting you know you're about to edit a symbol (**5.37**).

In isolation mode, you'll notice four dashed guides that run through the search box (**5.38**). You can move the lines to indicate which areas of the symbol will be resized and which will be protected when you transform the symbol.

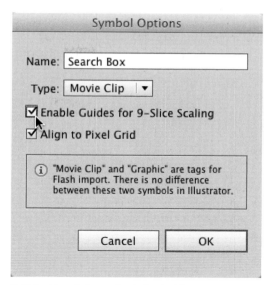

5.36 Enabling 9-slice scaling in Symbol Options

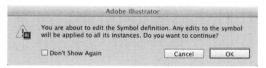

5.37 This warning lets you know that you have double-clicked a symbol and will enter isolation mode.

5.38 Guides for 9-slice scaling as shown in isolation mode

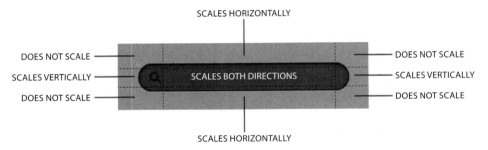

SCALES HORIZONTALLY

DOES NOT SCALE ———— ———— DOES NOT SCALE

SCALES VERTICALLY ———— SCALES BOTH DIRECTIONS ———— SCALES VERTICALLY

DOES NOT SCALE ———— ———— DOES NOT SCALE

SCALES HORIZONTALLY

5.39 How 9-slice scaling works

7. Place the guides in the search box as shown in **5.39**. Press Escape to exit isolation mode.

8. Select the Free Transform tool (E) and drag the right edge handle of the symbol to resize it.

   With the 9-slice scaling guides set, you can resize the search box without distorting the icon inside or the corners.

Going Off the Pixel Grid

Keeping objects on the pixel grid has been a major theme running throughout this chapter. The addition of pixel alignment features is what finally made Illustrator viable for UI design. However, it's still a drawing tool, and sometimes you'll want to include artwork that doesn't need to strictly adhere to the pixel grid.

Adding a few of these illustrative touches to your application UI will provide interest and variety. User interfaces don't have to be boring; if anything, they should always have some element of surprise and delight to help make an emotional connection with the user. It adds a human element into the mix.

Being that this is an app about toy cars, let's add some whimsical typographic touches to the page.

Creating an Application Logo

Wheelr needs a logo as an identifier. For this admittedly simple logo, I chose the font Clutchee, which is a free web font available at FontSquirrel (www.fontsquirrel.com). It's a bold display font that kind of looks like it has skid marks from a tire burnout running through each letter. Install the font on your system and then use it to create the logo.

NOTE If you're unsure how to install a new font on your computer, consult your operating system's help files for your installation instructions.

1. Select the Type tool (T) and click in the sidebar to create a point type object.

2. Type *Wheelr* and press Escape.

   This keyboard shortcut is indispensible when editing type. It quickly gets you out of type-editing mode, but leaves the type object selected.

3. Using the Control panel, set the font to Clutchee and size it to 42 pixels.

4. In the Control panel, click the Character link to pop up the Character panel. In the Tracking field , set the tracking value to *25*.

   A positive tracking value puts extra space between each letter, which helps the leg-ibility of this super-bold typeface.

5. Give it a white fill by clicking the white swatch in the Color panel.

6. Skewing the logo a little to the right makes it look speedy. To do this, click and hold the mouse on the Scale tool until the tool group flyout appears. Select the Shear tool from the group.

7. Double-click the Shear tool to bring up the Shear dialog box. Set the shear angle to 13 degrees and click OK.

8. Finish off the logo by placing it right at the top center of the sidebar (**5.40**).

9. Press ⌘S/Ctrl+S to save your work.

If you select this type object and view its posi-tion in the Transform panel, you'll notice that there are no whole pixel values to be seen. Because type objects are comprised of many curves and have font-specific data embedded that you can't change, they will never fit on the pixel grid. That's perfectly okay.

5.40 Final logo placement

Enhancing the Hierarchy

To emphasize the navigation hierarchy, you'll use a different typeface for the section headline, app navigation, and the Popular Collectors headline. Doing so will help to visually separate those section identifiers from the regular content. For these elements, use the free web font Komika Title, also available from FontSquirrel. I chose this typeface because it has a hand-lettered feel that's common with custom pinstriping and lettering. After you install it, use the font's Paint style to make the following changes:

1. Set the section headline, *The Latest,* to 18px Komika Title – Paint.

2. Set the *Collection*, *Crew*, and *Profile* navigation items to 13px Komika Title – Paint.

3. Set the *Popular Collectors* heading to 13px Komika Title – Paint.

4. Press ⌘S/Ctrl+S to save your work.

   Your final type should look like **5.41**.

5.41 The mockup is coming along nicely.

Using Layers for Organization

Much as you would layer ingredients to make the perfect BLT, you can use layers in Illustrator to stack your objects into logical groups. A BLT put in the blender probably wouldn't taste very good. In Illustrator, leaving all your objects on one layer is the equivalent scenario. Doing so makes it difficult to work with your design as it gets more complex.

To help with this organization principle, Illustrator provides the Layers panel (Window > Layers). You'll use the Layers panel in several ways to organize your art, and the panel itself has quite a few options. This section will outline the most useful features for UI design.

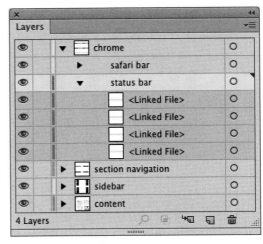

5.42 The Layers panel

The Layers Panel

The Layers panel (**5.42**) is, at its core, a list of all the objects in your document. By default, the panel contains a single parent layer with each object on the artboard listed underneath it. As you add objects to a layer, a triangle appears next to it that you can use to toggle the visibility of its contents in the panel. Each layer has a small thumbnail that gives you a visual representation of the objects that reside in it.

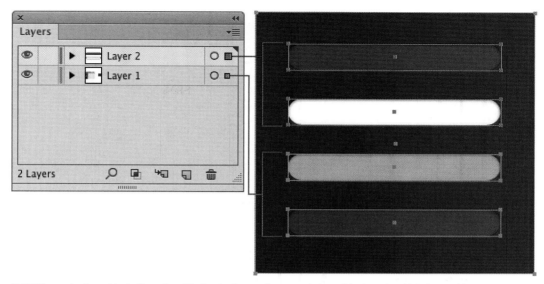

5.43 When selecting objects, the color of their selection outlines match that of the layer in which they reside.

You can add as many layers as you need to meet the needs of your design. Objects can be added to new layers and moved easily between them at any time. You can also reshuffle the stacking order of layers, which in turn affects how your objects display on the artboard. Each layer you create receives a color to help you identify its objects. When you select an object, its selection outline matches that of its parent layer (**5.43**).

Each item in the list has three columns that can be used for information about a layer or as a means of interacting with its objects. Clicking in a column controls the following layer characteristics:

• **Visibility:** Clicking in this column toggles the visibility of the layer contents. The presence of the Eye icon 👁 indicates that the objects on the layer are visible on the artboard.

- **Editability:** Clicking in this column toggles the editing capability of the layer. When the Lock icon 🔒 is present, the layer cannot be edited.

- **Selection:** This column indicates whether one or more items in the layer are selected. When all objects on the layer are selected, a large colored selection box appears in the column. If one or more items on the layer are unselected, the colored selection box is smaller (**5.44**).

5.44 The selection column indicates with a large colored square whether all objects on the layer are selected.

Display Options

The Layers panel has several different ways of displaying information. Your document's layer structure can be as simple or as complex as your needs and working style dictate. The panel provides viewing options for each type of workflow.

To change the display of the Layers panel, choose Panel Options from the Layers panel menu. The following options are available (**5.45**):

- **Show Layers Only:** This option hides from the list all the items that normally appear under a parent layer. I like to work this way since selecting objects on the artboard is really easy, and having all the cruft appear in the Layers panel just creates information overload.

- **Row Size:** As you begin to create a lot of layers, you might find that they take up a lot of space in the panel. You can make each row a preset size, or you can set a custom height.

- **Thumbnails:** You can select which thumbnails to show in the panel. The size of the thumbnail is determined by the row height set in the previous box. If you choose the Small row size, this Thumbnails option is disabled completely.

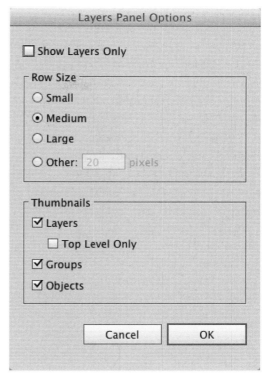

5.45 Layers Panel Options dialog box

Creating Layers

As you begin to make your designs more complex, using additional layers helps to organize your work into logical groups. Since you haven't gone too far into the Wheelr mockup yet, now would be a good time to do some housecleaning. My process for organizing artwork comes from my many years of working with Photoshop.

Typically, I create a layer for all background elements, one for the browser chrome, and then put the rest into layers based on where they fall in the page structure. For the Wheelr mockup, you'll create a header, sidebar, and content layer in addition to the two layers previously mentioned. To begin creating these layers and moving artwork to them:

1. Select Artboard 1 from the artboard navigator (found at the bottom left of the screen) to bring it into the view.

2. In the Layers panel, click the Create New Layer button to add a new layer to the list.

   New layers appear at the top of the list by default.

3. Rename this layer by double-clicking the name and typing *Chrome*. Additionally, rename the bottom layer *Background*.

4. Create three more layers and name them *Header, Sidebar,* and *Content* (**5.46**).

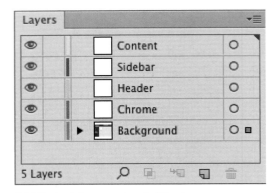

5.46 The basic layer structure for Wheelr

Moving Objects Between Layers

Now that the layer structure is in place, all you have left to do is populate the new layers. Right now, every piece of this design is on the Background layer. You'll change this by selecting the appropriate elements and moving them to their respective layers:

1. Select the browser chrome element with the Selection tool (V).

2. In the Layers panel, drag the colored selection square from Background to Chrome (**5.47**).

    Next, you'll move all the content to the header layer, independent of the background rectangles.

3. In the Layers panel, click the Selection column for the Background layer (**5.48**).

    This will select all the art on the background layer while leaving the chrome out of the selection. You'll need to deselect the background rectangles in order to move all the content.

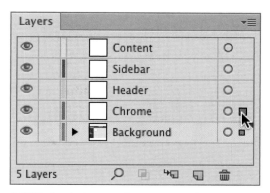

5.47 Moving the browser chrome to a new layer

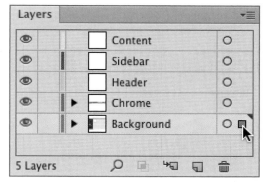

5.48 Click in the Selection column to select all objects on the layer.

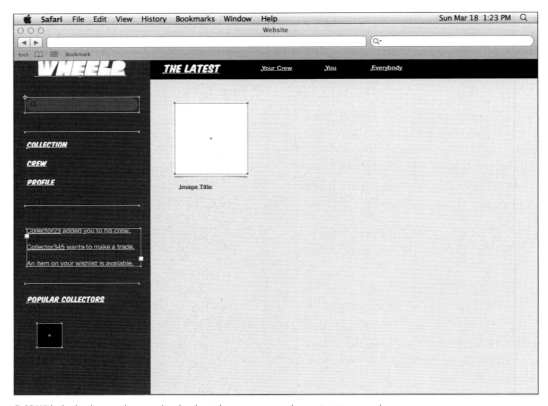

5.49 With the background rectangles deselected, you can move the content to a new layer.

4. Hold down the Shift key and click each of the background rectangles to remove them from the current selection (**5.49**).

   With the background shapes deselected, you can move all the text out of the Background layer.

5. Drag the colored selection square to the Header layer (**5.50**).

   Now that you have all the background elements and the browser chrome on their own layer, you can lock these layers to prevent them from being selected.

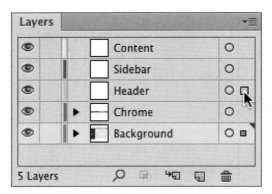

5.50 Moving content to the Header layer

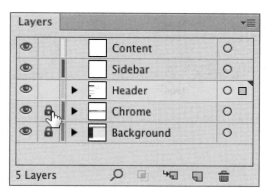

5.51 The lock icon indicates non-editable layers.

6. To lock the Background and Chrome layers, click the Lock column (**5.51**).

   The lock icon indicates that these layers are now unable to be selected or edited. Now you'll be able to easily select each grouping of content in order to move them to their respective layers.

7. With the Selection tool (V), click and drag around all the sidebar content (**5.52**). Move the colored selection square in the Layers panel to the Sidebar layer.

8. Select the photo frame and its label and move the colored selection square to the Content layer.

Now that all the content is organized into logical layers, let's take a moment to tighten up the layout before moving on to the next chapter.

5.52 Drag to select all the sidebar content as you prepare to move it to a new layer.

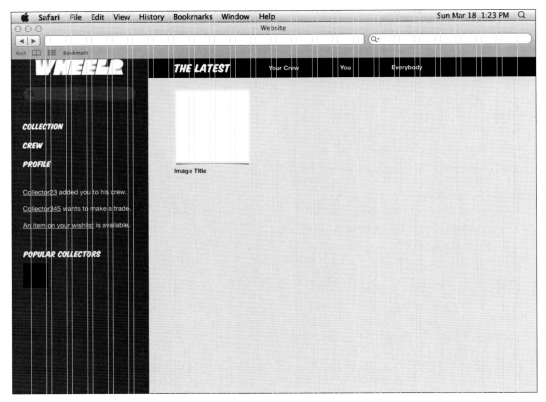

5.53 Use this as a guide for the tightened layout of elements in the mockup.

Tightening Up the Layout

Now that the structure is in place and you have all the necessary elements in the layout, let's put everything in its proper place. Up to this point, the content on the mockup has been placed pretty loosely. Depending on the level of fidelity you'll need for your client, you may choose to keep the layout loose or tighten it up substantially. I prefer to keep it somewhat loose until all the features and functionality get figured out, just in case there are changes.

Choose View Guides > Show Guides (⌘;/Ctrl+;) to make the grid visible again and then line up all the elements to roughly match **5.53**. Be sure to press ⌘S/Ctrl+S to save your work when you are done.

Conclusion

The Appearance panel makes it possible to create beautiful graphics using multiple layers and effects using a single object. You can edit these effects at any time without affecting the original object. You can then take the design and save it as a graphic style that can be used on other objects.

Symbols allow you to create multiple instances of an object or group of objects. They can be used to create common interface elements like search boxes, icons, buttons, and even entire backgrounds. 9-slice scaling allows symbols to be resized while keeping their corners intact.

Layers give you the ability to organize your artwork into logical groupings. This can assist in making selections, showing and hiding certain pieces of the design for simplicity, and protecting areas you don't want to accidentally edit.

Creativity and efficiency are the name of the game here, and these features give you the best of both worlds. The next chapter aims to take them a step further by introducing more effects for graphic styles, symbols, as well as additional features for text. You'll also learn how to work with images.

WHEELZ

THE LATEST

Your Crew   You

COLLECTION

CREW

PROFILE

Collector23 added you to his crew.

Collector345 wants to make a trade.

An item on your wishlist is available.

Image Title   Image Title   Image Title

6

FINISHING TOUCHES

Chapter Overview

So far, you've covered the basics and should be well on your way to discovering Illustrator's potential as a competent UI design tool. In this chapter, you'll delve into a few more advanced features that will help put the finishing touches on the mockup. The topics covered in this chapter include the following:

- Using Illustrator and Photoshop Effects
- Applying additional type techniques
- Working with images

Taking Appearances to the Next Level

In the last chapter, you learned how to use the Appearance panel to craft a fairly complex widget from just one object. That appearance can then be saved and applied to any other vector object in your document. Where this provides the most benefit is in documents that have multiple screens.

As you begin to add complexity to your design, saving those appearances for reuse increases efficiency by allowing you to apply styles and make changes really quickly, thereby increasing your ability to get more done in less time.

Let's take a look at some advanced techniques with the Appearance panel and graphic styles.

Illustrator and Photoshop Effects

First, let's delve into a little history. Many moons ago, Illustrator (a vector application) and Photoshop (a raster application) existed as completely separate products in every way. If I needed a logo that could scale to any size without any degradation, I knew I could count on Illustrator to come through. If there was a need for a photo composition that relied on special effects, photo filters, and textures, Photoshop was the tool for the job.

Then something happened. Over time, both programs gained from each other bits of native functionality you used to have to cut and paste from one app to the other to achieve. For example, it was a major leap when Photoshop gained vector shape tools and type. I could create elements in Photoshop I could resize without a loss of quality. It was amazing.

But what really floored me was when Illustrator acquired the ability to use many of Photoshop's filters on vector objects. That seemed like such a huge jump; I could now add a drop shadow in Illustrator without having to cut and paste between the two applications. The time and effort saved by these additions was incredible.

This chapter shows you how to use this functionality to improve the design of certain elements within the Wheelr mockup, and how to use it in your own UI design projects. You'll start by digging into the Effect menu, where you'll notice two distinct divisions, Illustrator Effects and Photoshop Effects (**6.1**). The majority of these effects are tailor-made for illustration purposes, but a few of each are useful for UI design:

- Convert To Shape

- Distort & Transform > Transform

- Path

- Rasterize

- Stylize

- Artistic > Film Grain

- Blur

- Texture > Grain

- Texture > Texturizer

6.1 Illustrator and Photoshop Effects in the Effect menu

NOTE In case you opened the book to this chapter without reading any of the previous ones, the mockup mentioned in this chapter was started back in Chapter 4. I encourage you to go back and follow along through Chapters 4 and 5 to get more out of this exercise.

The main difference between Illustrator and Photoshop effects are as follows:

- **Illustrator Effects are resolution-independent.** Any object that has an Illustrator effect applied can be scaled with no loss of quality. When you resize an object, Illustrator does the math for you and scales the effect to match. Most Illustrator effects tend to be more vector-based anyway, with the exception of Drop Shadow, Inner Glow, Outer Glow, and Feather.

- **Photoshop effects are not resolution-independent.** They're rendered at the settings found in the Document Raster Effects Settings (DRES), which is also accessed from the Effect menu. If an object is scaled that has a Photoshop effect applied, the effect scales, but remains at the resolution setting in the DRES.

For Photoshop effects, you can use the DRES to set the resolution to match that of your target device, or you can use the settings to optimize the appearance of the effect. You'll see how this works later in the chapter. For now, let's look at how you can use the most common Illustrator effects in the Wheelr mockup.

Using Illustrator's Stylize Effects

You may have realized by now that you already used five Illustrator effects (Round Corners, Inner Glow and Drop Shadow, Distort & Transform, and Warp) when you created the search box and photo frame in Chapter 5. You'll try some other examples to create a landing page for Wheelr.

Turbocharge your collection.

Whether you've been collecting die-cast cars for years or are just getting started, Wheelr can help you curate and manage your collection, discover new models, and buy, sell, trade and connect with a vibrant and active community. It's free to use and easy to get started. Just click one of the buttons to the right to sign up with your Twitter or Facebook account to try Wheelr today!

Sign up with your Twitter account

Sign up with your Facebook account

Blog About Contact Privacy Policy Terms

6.2 Wheelr's landing page

Most applications have a landing page as the first thing a prospective user sees. It serves to advertise the features and benefits of the product. A landing page is an essential marketing tool that helps a prospective user to decide whether or not to use your app. I've started a simple one for you to enhance. To follow along, download the starter file at www.peachpit.com/UIwithAI/chp6/landingpage.ai.

This is an extremely basic landing page (**6.2**) that provides a description of the product and a way to quickly get signed up for the service. When you've finished with the exercises, play around with the design to see how you might make this landing page even more effective.

Begin by styling the sign-up buttons. These buttons act as a call to action on the page, giving the viewer a clear idea as to what can be done. The buttons might be effective in their current state, but you'll make them look more clickable than they do right now:

1. Select the Twitter sign-up button and click the Path layer in the Appearance panel.

2. Choose Effect > Stylize > Round Corners and enter *5 px* as the value in the Round Corners dialog box.

3. Select the Fill layer and then choose Effect > Stylize > Drop Shadow.

4. In the Drop Shadow dialog box, choose Normal mode, 35% Opacity, an X offset of 0, a Y Offset of 1 px, and a Blur value of 3 px. If the color is not already set to #000000 (black), click the color swatch and make it so (**6.3**). Click OK.

At this point, this looks like a clickable button (**6.4**). Round corners serve to draw the eye into the button and its content rather than pointing outside of it. It relieves the visual tension that can be created sometimes by sharp corners. The drop shadow pops the button off the page and reinforces its clickability.

Next, you'll give the button content an inset look to add a little more visual weight to it.

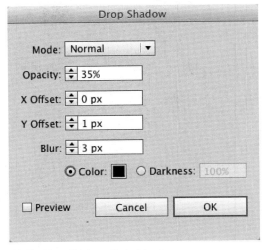

6.3 The Drop Shadow effect dialog box

6.4 Making a nice button

5. Select the Twitter bird logo and the button text. In the Appearance panel, the selection will show as Mixed Objects (**6.5**).

6. Choose Effect > Stylize > Drop Shadow.

7. In the dialog box that appears, change the Opacity to 50%, the Y Offset to 2 px, the Blur value to 0, and the color to #ffffff (white). Click OK.

   This effect makes the content look like it's carved into the button (**6.6**). It adds to the realistic appearance by making the button seem three-dimensional. The next step is to save these appearances as graphic styles so you can apply them to the other button.

8. With the Twitter button still selected, choose New Graphic Style from the Graphic Styles panel menu. (You can access the Graphic Styles panel by choose Window > Graphic Styles.) Be sure to give this new style an appropriate name. Click OK.

9. Select the text on the Twitter button and create a new graphic style using the instructions in the previous step. Name this graphic style *2px white drop shadow*.

   When you create a graphic style from a text object, Illustrator does not pull any text-formatting attributes. In this case, it saves only the white drop shadow in the style. This is a good thing, as you'll see in a moment.

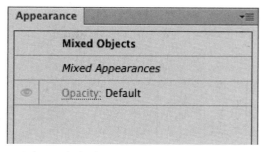

6.5 When multiple objects with different attributes are selected, the Appearance panel shows them as Mixed Objects.

6.6 The finished button

TIP You can also add a new style by clicking the New Graphic Style button ⬚ at the bottom of the panel. However, using the command in the panel menu lets you name the new style as you create it. Otherwise, you'll have to double-click the style in the panel to change the name.

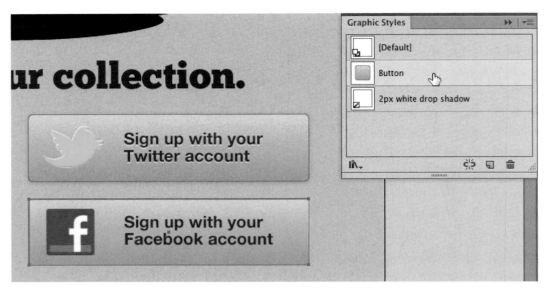

6.7 Applying a graphic style

Applying Graphic Styles to Additional Objects

Now that the styling of that button is complete, you can use the graphic styles you just created to style the other button and its content.

1. Select the Facebook button and click the button style in the Graphic Styles panel (**6.7**).

2. Select the Facebook logo and the text in the button and click the white drop shadow style.

   Because the white drop shadow style didn't have any text-formatting attributes, you were able to apply it to both the logo and the text at the same time. You'd be able to apply this drop shadow to any other text and it would retain its formatting as well.

How easy was that (**6.8**)? Graphic styles really do make the task of designing for consistency drop-dead simple.

6.8 The finished set of buttons on the landing page

6.9 Landing page header, pre-style

Adding Old-School Style to the Page Header

Next, you'll move on to styling the flame in the header of the page (**6.9**). The flame is inside a mask that hides everything outside the black box. The inspiration for this flame graphic is the pinstriped and airbrushed look you might see on an old hot rod (**6.10**). I'd like to have the flame be more subtle than the one in the photo, so you'll ignore the background color from the flame and just do a glow on the inside. You'll use an Illustrator effect to make it a little more interesting:

1. Double-click the flame graphic to enter isolation mode. If you've disabled this feature, right-click the graphic and choose Isolate Selected Clipping Mask. Select the flame artwork and remove the yellow stroke. (It was there only for preview purposes.)

2. Click the fill layer in the Appearance panel and choose Effect > Stylize > Inner Glow.

3. In the dialog box, select Screen mode and give it a fill of #f2ec33. Set the Opacity to 75%, and make the Blur 24 px (**6.11**). Click OK and then press Escape to exit isolation mode.

6.10 The flames on this old truck provided the inspiration for the landing page header. Photo by Rick Moore.

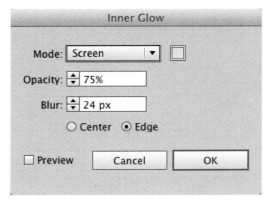

6.11 Inner Glow settings

6.12 Header flame with Inner Glow effect added

That looks pretty good for now (**6.12**). You'll make it look even better in the next section.

Using Photoshop Effects

Photoshop effects are nice to have around as they can help add texture and depth that would be difficult to do with a purely vector approach. In the old days, you'd have to go into Photoshop, create the textured effects needed for the design, and then import them into Illustrator. It got the job done, but ultimately, that method was both time-consuming and inflexible. Any changes that needed to be made often meant that the textured effect would have to be recreated each time.

Those days are long gone. For all but the most complicated effects, you can use Illustrator's Photoshop Effects to achieve the look you are after. There are quite a few effects included with Illustrator, and what's really cool is that you can load third-party filters into Illustrator as well. If you're a Photoshop user who has invested heavily in filters and effects, you'll be pleased to discover that they can serve double duty.

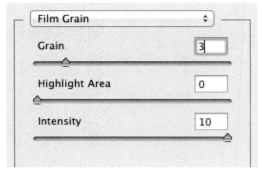

6.13 Film Grain effect settings

Let's go back to the flame graphic and punch it up a bit. I love old cars that have metallic flake paint jobs. I think it would look great to add that texture into the background behind the flames. The little sparkles in the paint would be really time-consuming to complete with pure vector artwork, so you'll use a Photoshop effect to pull off the look.

1. With the Direct Selection tool ![cursor] (A), select the black background just behind the flame and then click the fill layer in the Appearance panel.

2. Choose Effect > Artistic > Film Grain.

3. In the Film Grain effect setting pane, set the Grain setting to 3 (**6.13**). Click OK.

6.14 Flame header with grain added to simulate metal-flake paint

6.15 The finished landing page

The grain makes the black background look like a metallic paint, and having the Screen blend mode set on the flame allows the grain to show through (**6.14**). I think it looks fantastic. Now, apply the same effect to the gray page background:

4. Select the gray background object and apply the Film Grain effect to it. Use a Grain setting of 2 for this object. Click OK.

    The textured background helps the content to pop, giving it a good balance with the large red car at the top of the page. The buttons really stand out now, which is important for a call to action (**6.15**).

Effect Gallery

When selecting some Photoshop effects, a super-sized dialog box called the Effect Gallery appears (**6.16**). Basically, it provides the convenience of being able to preview each available effect before you apply it. The left side of the dialog box is for the effect preview. The center pane houses the effects, categorized by type. The settings for each effect are accessed in the right pane.

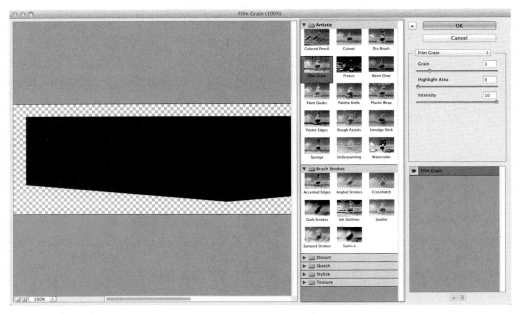

6.16 The Effect Gallery

6.17 The mockup with texture effects applied

Let's move back to the Wheelr application mockup. Repeat the grain texture from the landing page to the background of the sidebar, section navigation bar, and content area. Doing so helps to create consistency in the design. Add the Film Grain effect to the sidebar, section navigation, and main content rectangles as described in the previous steps. Use a Grain setting of 1 for the sidebar, and 2 for the section navigation and content area (**6.17**).

NOTE You can download the project file for this section's examples at www.peachpit.com/UIwithAI/ch6/wheelr6.ai.

The shadow on the photo box needs to be softened a little to help it look more like a real shadow. Here is how you can use an effect to do that:

1. Select the photo box and click the bottom fill layer in the Appearance panel.

2. Choose Effect > Blur > Gaussian Blur.

3. Set the Radius for the effect to 1.5 and click OK.

   The Gaussian Blur effect softens the edge of the object to the specified pixel radius. The larger the radius value is, the softer the shadow. A small number was used in this case so that the photo frame doesn't appear as if it's hovering too far off the background (**6.18**).

Understanding Document Raster Effects Settings

The Document Raster Effects Settings (DRES) determine the resolution for Photoshop Effects applied to your artwork. You can access the settings from the Effect menu. The dialog box (**6.19**) allows you to choose from three resolution settings (72, 150, or 300 ppi). You can also enter an arbitrary number by choosing Other from the Resolution pop-up menu.

6.18 Using Gaussian blur to soften the photo frame drop shadow

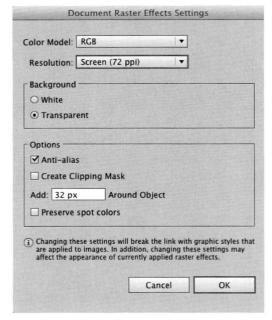

6.19 The Document Raster Effects Settings dialog box

When you apply a Photoshop effect to an object, it will look different depending on what resolution you have set in the DRES. For example, you used the Film Grain effect on the sidebar background in the Wheelr mockup. **6.20** shows what that effect looks like in each of the three preset resolutions (in regular Preview mode, viewed at 600%). At lower resolution settings, the effect looks coarser because of the fewer number of pixels. As you get to 300 ppi, the effect is almost imperceptible, at least to my old eyes.

What resolution you use is really up to you and how you want the object to look in the final design, as well as how you plan to use it in the long term. If you plan to use it only onscreen, 72 ppi is probably good enough, provided you achieve the look you want. After all, when using Photoshop effects, what you see on the screen is what you will get when you export your art for final use. However, if you plan to repurpose the graphic for print, you may want to consider using a higher resolution and adjusting the settings to match your visual needs.

One important thing to note if you decide to change the resolution settings: Increasing or decreasing the DRES affects *any* object in your document that has a raster effect applied. That means it may negatively change the appearance of effects with which you are already satisfied. However, there is a way around this limitation: using the Rasterize effect.

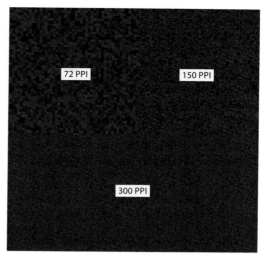

6.20 Film Grain effect at 72, 150, and 300 ppi

The Rasterize effect turns a vector object into a bitmap one. Illustrator has been able to do this for years, but it was a destructive effect; once it was applied, using undo was the only way to restore the object to a vector. Now you can use Rasterize as a live effect, which allows you to change the resolution of a single object on the artboard, rather than changing the DRES and affecting all objects. Here's how it works:

1. In the Wheelr mockup, select the background rectangle of the sidebar. This had the Film Grain effect applied previously. Unless you changed it at some point, the DRES for this document is the default 72 ppi.

2. In the Appearance panel, select the fill layer.

3. Choose Effect > Rasterize.

   The Rasterize dialog box appears, looking almost exactly like the DRES dialog box (**6.21**).

4. Change the Resolution to High (300 ppi) and choose Art Optimized (Supersampling) from the Anti-aliasing pop-up menu. Click OK.

5. Drag the Rasterize effect above the Film Grain layer to have it apply correctly (**6.22**).

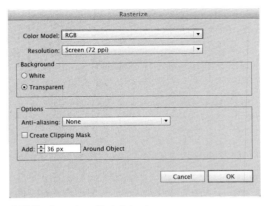

6.21 The Rasterize effect dialog box

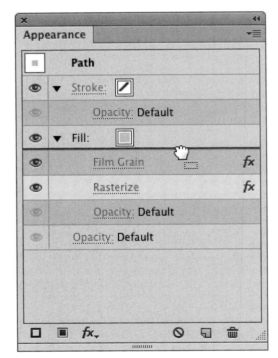

6.22 The Rasterize effect needs to be the top layer in order to be effective.

After a second or two, you'll see the film grain almost disappear. It's still there; it's just at a much higher resolution now. The important thing to notice is that the other Film Grain effects on the artboard have not changed (**6.23**). This is an important feature, because it allows you to tailor raster effects at the object level so that they look exactly as you want them.

Since you don't really want to make that grainy texture disappear, you'll need to get rid of the Rasterize effect on the sidebar. Instead of using the traditional undo (⌘Z/ Ctrl+Z), select the sidebar in the Appearance panel and drag the unwanted effect to the panel's Trash icon 🗑.

6.23 The Film Grain effect on the sidebar is almost imperceptible at 300 ppi.

Additional Rasterizing Options

In the Rasterize effect dialog box, you also have the option to use a clipping path on the object or add space around the object (**6.24**). Certain raster effects, like Gaussian blur, take up space outside the object; others are constrained to the object dimensions. The additional settings allow you to give the effect the space it needs in order to look right.

To create a clipping mask as you apply the Rasterize effect, simply select the option in the effect dialog box. The path will hide anything outside the bounds of the object, which can be useful as some raster effects add weird pixels to the edges as they're applied.

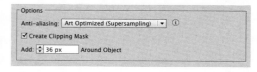

6.24 Rasterization options

To add up to 720 pixels of space around an object, enter the number of pixels to add in the text field. The default amount of space added around the object is 36 pixels. Adding space is most useful with Blur effects, as they go outside the bounds of the object.

Additive Styles

So far you have learned to create a graphic style that comprises several appearance attributes. When applied to another object on the artboard, that object takes on all the attributes of the style, replacing any that it currently had. But you can also apply a graphic style to an object without replacing the current appearance. These are called additive styles.

Additive styles are useful when you need to add an appearance attribute to an object without changing its current look. One example would be to use an additive style to give a soft drop shadow to an object that already has a graphic style applied. A second example would be to create a step-and-repeat effect, which makes offset copies of a single object.

The best way to create an additive style is to make a new style that is not based on any selected objects. Because of that, you won't see any change on the artboard as you create the style. To see how this works, you'll create a style that will be used to generate several offset copies of the photo frame, its label, and the *Popular Collectors* section thumbnail, all in the Wheelr mockup. Follow these steps to create the additive style:

1. Choose Select > Deselect (⌘⇧A/ Ctrl+Shift+A) to make sure you have nothing selected on the artboard.

2. From the Appearance panel menu, choose Clear Appearance to remove any attributes that might remain from a previously selected object, allowing you to start with a clean slate.

3. Choose Effect > Distort & Transform > Transform.

4. In the Transform Effect dialog box, set the Horizontal value in the Move section to 160 px, and the Copies value to 1 (**6.25**). Click OK.

   When this effect is eventually applied to an object, it will offset a copy of that original object 160 pixels to the right.

5. Choose Effect > Distort & Transform > Transform to add a second effect to this style. You'll most likely be warned that you are about to add another instance of this effect (**6.26**). Click Apply New Effect.

6. In the Transform Effect dialog box, set the Vertical value in the Move section to 201 px, and the Copies value to 1. Click OK.

   Again, when this effect is eventually applied to an object, it offsets another copy of the object 201 pixels below the original.

7. In the Graphic Styles panel, click the New Graphic Style button 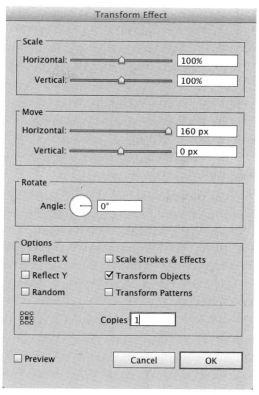 and then double-click the name to rename it *Step and Repeat*.

   When this graphic style is applied, it will use both Transform effects to create two offset copies of the selected object at the same time.

6.25 The Transform Effect settings dialog box

6.26 Applying another effect makes a warning dialog box appear, just in case you didn't mean to add another effect.

NOTE The number to specify is not arbitrary; you'll actually need to do a little math to figure out how far you want to offset the object. In this example, I know that I am going to use the 142-pixel-wide photo frame, which has a 4-pixel border. The border adds 4 pixels to each side of the frame, adding up to a 150-pixel-wide frame. I'd like 10 pixels of space between frames (to match the gutters in the grid), so the final number is 160 pixels.

NOTE If you want to edit the effect parameters, click the effect link in the Appearance panel. In this example, you really do want two instances of the effect.

You can now add this step-and-repeat effect to any object on the artboard, including objects that already have a graphic style applied. Let's see how this works on the photo frame as an additive style.

1. Select the photo frame and click the Step and Repeat style in the Graphic Styles panel while pressing Option/Alt.

   The additive style first creates the horizontal copy and then the vertical copy. By doing so, you end up with four squares (**6.27**). The blue selection outline shows that this is one object with three virtual copies. If you click one of the copies, Illustrator selects the original object. If you try to move the original, all the copies move with it. It makes dealing with a large number of identical objects really easy. Now, you'll fill out the rest of the content area by editing the number of copies.

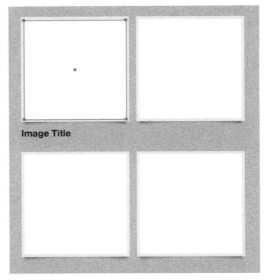

6.27 Applying the step-and-repeat style to an object

2. With the original photo frame selected, click each of the Transform effect links in the Appearance panel and respectively set the number of horizontal copies to 3 and the number of vertical copies to 2.

   All that is left to do is step-and-repeat the photo frame label and the Popular Collectors thumbnail image.

3. Select the label and click the Step and Repeat style to copy it, and then add the extra copies using the instructions in the previous step. **6.28** shows the result.

4. Select the black square under the *Popular Collectors* headline in the sidebar and add three horizontal and three vertical copies to it using the same instructions from step 2. **6.29** shows the result.

5. Press ⌘S/Ctrl+S to save your work.

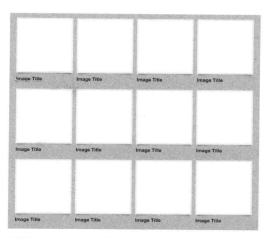

6.28 Step-and-repeat the photo frame labels

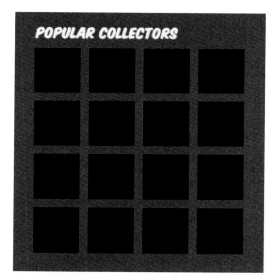

6.29 Applying the step-and-repeat style to another object

Additional Type Techniques

One thing I love about Illustrator is how easy it makes working with type. Being able to place, select, and edit type easily makes the design process much more enjoyable. In Chapter 4, you were introduced to the basics of Illustrator's Type tools. Several more features in addition to those can be used effectively in a UI design workflow.

Getting Text into Illustrator

In order to format and design content, you need to have some content. So far, we have worked with very small amounts of text in Wheelr. But if you're designing an app that will deal with large amounts of text, Illustrator has great features for dealing with that, too.

The first issue is getting text into Illustrator. There are several ways to do this. The first is to type all the content yourself. If you're like me and avoided typing or keyboarding classes in high school, that option is probably not at the top of your list. (And here I am writing a book, using my finely honed hunt-and-peck typing technique. Ugh.)

The second is to import your type from another source. Illustrator imports the following file formats:

- Microsoft Word for Windows 97, 98, 2000, 2002, 2003, and 2007

- Microsoft Word for Mac OS X, 2004, and 2008

- RTF (Rich Text Format)

- Plain text (ASCII) with ANSI, Unicode, Shift JIS, GB2312, Chinese Big 5, Cyrillic, GB18030, Greek, Turkish, Baltic, and Central European encoding

You can also copy and paste text from another source, but if you import from a file, the text retains all its character and paragraph formatting. Any character and paragraph styles in the Word or RTF document are imported into their respective panels in Illustrator, which can be a big help if the content creator has created font and style specifications previously.

I created a simple Word document you can download from www.peachpit.com/UIwithAI/ch6/dummytext.doc. You can use this file to see how importing text works. To import the contents of this text file into your document:

1. Open a new document and choose File > Place.

2. In the dialog box, navigate to the file on your hard disk and click Place.

   When importing a Word document or an RTF file, a secondary dialog box will appear asking you to specify which document extras to include and whether to remove text formatting. If you're importing a Plain Text file, you'll get a secondary dialog box that will allow you to set the encoding parameters as well as specify spacing and carriage return options.

   Illustrator places the contents of the file in an Area type box large enough to fit in the current artboard (**6.30**).

6.30 Imported text

From there, you can edit this text like you would any other text container in Illustrator.

Sometimes you won't have content to work with as you begin the design process. Although this definitely isn't ideal, not every organization has the resources or capability to do full-scale content strategy before the design process begins, so you have to make do. If this is the case, you can use dummy text to flesh out the content areas in your design. If you know how to speak fake Latin (it's a lost art), I'm jealous of your head start. But if you don't, a couple of cool resources can get you any quantity of dummy text you need. The best cross-platform solution I have found is Lipsum (www.lipsum.com). It's a web-based tool that allows you to generate any number of words, paragraphs, or lists for your layout. If you need a tool that doesn't rely on a web connection, there is Lipservice (www.lipserviceapp.com) for Windows or LittleIpsum (www.littleipsum.com or the Mac App Store) for Macintosh. Both are free applications that copy user-specified amounts of dummy text to the clipboard. Again, use these only if you're unable to get real content from your team or customer. It's always better to know and understand the content of your site or app, as it helps to inform the design.

Area Type Options

Once you've imported your text into Illustrator, you'll find several ways to edit it. Remember that area type is constrained to a user-specified container, allowing you to create blocks of type in your design. When designing user interfaces, you'll discover that area type works best for areas where you need to relinquish control for how text wraps. To simulate text wrapping with point type, you would have to insert hard returns at the end of each line to create a block of text. If the column size were to change in any way, the text wrapping would break. That creates more work than necessary.

Using area type helps alleviate that extra work by handling the wrapping for you. For example, if you were designing an application for reading content from blog feeds, area type would be a great choice for visualizing how that content might fit within the screen design. If the container size changes, the type wraps accordingly. The size of the browser window determines the wrapping anyway, so why fight it?

Resizing blocks of area type is very simple. There are two ways to go about it:

- Resize one side or point at a time by using the Direct Selection tool (A) and dragging points or segments of the type container. The cursor changes as you drag the segment (**6.31**).

- Choose Type > Area Type Options and adjust the settings (**6.32**) to get fine-grained control over height, width, and even inset values.

One thing you should never do is use the Free Transform tool to resize an area type container. Doing so distorts the type inside by stretching or condensing it. There is no greater travesty in this world than artificially distorted type (**6.33**). Well, I'm exaggerating, but it is pretty bad.

Curabitur blandit tempus porttitor. Fusce dapibus, tellus ac cursus commodo, tortor mauris condimentum nibh, ut fermentum massa justo sit amet risus. Maecenas faucibus mollis interdum. Vestibulum id ligula porta felis euismod semper. Vivamus sagittis lacus vel augue laoreet rutrum faucibus dolor auctor.

Duis mollis, est non commodo luctus, nisi erat porttitor ligula, eget lacinia odio sem nec elit. Aenean lacinia bibendum nulla sed consectetur. Vestibulum id ligula porta felis euismod semper. Cras mattis consectetur purus sit amet fermentum.

Donec sed odio dui. Integer posuere erat a ante venenatis dapibus posuere velit aliquet. Sed posuere consectetur est at lobortis. Donec sed odio dui. Vestibulum id ligula porta felis euismod semper. Cum sociis natoque penatibus et magnis dis parturient montes, nascetur ridiculus mus. Donec sed odio dui.

6.31 Using the Direct Selection tool to resize an area type container

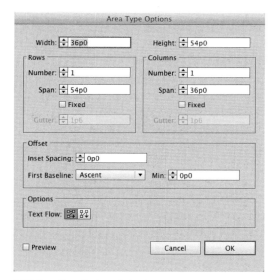

6.32 Area Type Options dialog box

6.33 Don't ever do this. Please.

Nulla vitae elit libero, a pharetra augue. Donec sed odio dui. Etiam porta sem malesuada magna mollis euismod. Donec sed odio dui. Integer posuere erat a ante venenatis dapibus posuere velit aliquet. Etiam porta sem malesuada magna mollis euismod. Cras justo odio, dapibus ac facilisis in, egestas eget quam.

Aenean eu leo quam. Pellentesque ornare sem lacinia quam venenatis vestibulum. Nulla vitae elit libero, a pharetra augue. Etiam porta sem malesuada magna mollis euismod. Integer posuere erat a ante venenatis dapibus posuere velit aliquet. Vestibulum id ligula porta felis euismod semper. Aenean lacinia bibendum nulla consectetur. Cum sociis natoque penatibus et magnis parturient montes, nascetur ridiculus mus.

Curabitur blandit tempus porttitor. Vivamus sagittis lacus vel augue laoreet rutrum faucibus dolor auctor. Donec ullamcorper nulla non metus auctor fringilla. Etiam porta sem malesuada magna mollis euismod.

Aenean lacinia bibendum nulla sed consectetur. Nullam quis risus eget urna mollis ornare vel eu leo. Donec ullamcorper nulla non metus auctor fringilla. Lorem ipsum dolor sit amet, consectetur adipiscing elit.

6.34 Working with text wraps

Simulating Floats

A float is a CSS property used to push content away from an image or other object in the layout. Floats have their roots in print where images are used to break up long passages of text, to help provide context, or to create interest and variety on the page. Floats are also used to create multicolumn layouts in HTML and CSS.

Illustrator has a feature that will help you to simulate floats in your design. Specifically,

you can use the Text Wrap feature to help content flow around an image or graphic object. This feature places an invisible wall around an object that pushes all text aside. Once the text wrap has been set, you can change the object's position and the text will always flow around it. Creating a text wrap is really easy. To follow along, download the file (**6.34**) from www.peachpit.com/UIwithAI/ch6/text-wrap.ai.

Nulla vitae elit libero, a pharetra augue. Donec sed odio dui. Etiam porta sem malesuada magna mollis euismod. Donec sed odio dui. Integer posuere erat a ante venenatis dapibus posuere velit aliquet. Etiam porta sem malesuada magna mollis euismod. Cras justo odio, dapibus ac facilisis in, egestas eget quam.

Aenean eu leo quam. Pellentesque ornare sem lacinia quam venenatis vestibulum. Nulla vitae elit libero, a pharetra augue. Etiam porta sem malesuada magna mollis euismod. Integer posuere erat a ante venenatis dapibus posuere velit aliquet. Vestibulum id ligula porta felis euismod semper. Aenean lacinia bibendum nulla sed consectetur. Cum sociis natoque penatibus et magnis dis parturient montes, nascetur ridiculus mus.

Curabitur blandit tempus porttitor. Vivamus sagittis lacus vel augue laoreet rutrum faucibus dolor auctor. Donec ullamcorper nulla non metus auctor fringilla. Etiam porta sem malesuada magna mollis euismod.

Aenean lacinia bibendum nulla sed consectetur. Nullam⊞

6.35 The image with the text wrap applied

The file has a text area and an image. To create a text wrap, perform the following steps:

1. Select the image you want to float. Make sure that it is in front of the text by choosing Object > Arrange > Bring to Front (⌘⇧]/Ctrl+Shift+]).

2. Choose Object > Text Wrap > Make.

   Your text now flows around the image (**6.35**). You can adjust the margin around the image by choosing Object > Text Wrap > Text Wrap Options and adjusting the Offset value.

TIP To turn off text wrapping, select the image and then choose Object > Text Wrap > Release.

Creating a Drop Cap

You can take the text wrap a step further by creating a drop cap using the same steps. Drop caps are a great stylistic alternative when you want to direct a reader's eye to the beginning of the content. Illustrator doesn't have a drop cap command yet, but you can use a text wrap to quickly create one:

1. Double-click the text block, select the first letter, and choose Edit > Cut (⌘X/Ctrl+X) to cut it to the clipboard.

2. While pressing ⌘/Ctrl, drag to create an area type box, and then choose Edit > Paste (⌘V/Ctrl+V) to paste the letter from the clipboard (**6.36**).

You could use either point or area type for this step, but I prefer area type so that the text wraps around the box and not the character.

3. Format your letter to make it big and bold, and then apply the text wrap by choosing Object > Text Wrap > Make. Move it into place at the front of the paragraph so the text flows around it.

Just like the previous image, you can change the size and position of the drop cap and the text will always flow around it (**6.37**).

6.36 Cut and paste the first letter into a separate area type container.

6.37 The final drop cap

Using Find and Replace

If you've ever used a word processor to do anything more than type a letter or grocery list, you've probably discovered its find and replace feature. Find and replace allows you to find a character, word, or phrase in the text and replace it with something else. It's great for when you have to swap out a wrong word, correct adjusted nomenclature, or change certain hyphens to en dashes. It's a humongous timesaver.

After using Illustrator for several years, I discovered that it, too, has a find and replace feature. When working on a UI design with several artboards, find and replace allows you to work much more efficiently than making common text changes manually. It's a pretty powerful feature and one that you should know how to take advantage of in your work.

Here's how it works:

1. Using the **text-wrap.ai** file from the previous section, choose Edit > Find and Replace.

    You're going to use the feature to find all the instances of *nulla* and change them to *nullam*. (Again, if you can read fake Latin, you're golden!)

2. Enter *nulla* in the Find field. Be sure to enter it in all lowercase.

3. Enter *nullam* in the Replace With field. As before, use all lowercase letters.

    At this point, you'll notice that the only actions you can take with this dialog box are to click Find or Done (**6.38**). That's because you can't replace anything in the text until Illustrator knows that what you're looking for is actually there.

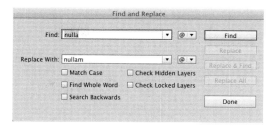

6.38 The Find and Replace dialog box

4. Click Find.

   If Illustrator finds the word, it jumps to and highlights the text. The other buttons also become enabled in the dialog box (**6.39**).

Once Illustrator has found your text, you have several options:

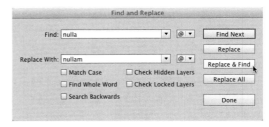

6.39 Find and Replace with all options available

- Click **Find Next** to cycle through all instances of the word in your document.

- Click **Replace** to replace the currently selected word.

- Click **Replace & Find** to replace the currently selected word and then select the next instance. This option lets you see what will be changed before you commit to changing it. That way you don't accidentally replace a word that you didn't mean to.

- Click **Replace All** to replace all instances of the word. This option replaces all instances automatically. Although it automates the process completely, it may end up making unwanted changes. Use it with caution.

   Several options let you refine the selection. These can be very helpful in complex documents. You can also use find and replace to change certain characters such as bullets, tab characters, or quotation marks by selecting them from the @ pop-up menu.

5. When you're finished with the Find and Replace dialog box, click Done.

Working with Images

UIs don't have to be all spreadsheets, icons, and commands. Photographic images can provide color and life to your application interfaces. Even though Illustrator is a vector program, you'll find that it handles images adequately. You can do basic image processing (color correction and color conversion), as well as performing basic transformations and Photoshop effects applications.

Images can either be linked to the original or embedded in the document. Each method has pros and cons. Linking images keeps the Illustrator document size small. It also allows you to edit the original in your image editor at any time and have it update in Illustrator. The only con to this method is that you need to keep all your external images and include them with the Illustrator file if you distribute it to someone else. This can get a little complicated if you are using a lot of images, because if you forget to include an image, it won't show up if someone else opens the file.

Embedding images allows you to get rid of the originals and keep everything in one place, but at the expense of losing editing and bloating the file size. Personally, I find it easier to link images that would be difficult to recreate (like an original photo) or images that are really large. Then I embed all the rest. It really comes down to preference and what works best for your workflow.

Preparing Images for Import

There are several best practices to keep in mind when getting images ready for import into Illustrator. Following these practices will help keep your file sizes small and your workflow efficient. Since Illustrator is not an image-editing application, it's best to leave these features to an app like Photoshop. The following suggestions are important to remember when preparing images:

- Size images in an image editor to the dimensions they will be used in your mockup. Trying to reduce or enlarge images in Illustrator doesn't help with image quality and can add a lot or extra weight to both the file size and the amount of memory the app uses (**6.40**). This can cause slowdowns in performance and increases the risk of untimely crashes.

- Crop, rotate, and flip images in your image editor before bringing them into Illustrator. Again, make Photoshop do all these image calculations for you, not Illustrator. You'll be better off in the long run.

- Take care of any color correction and image fidelity issues beforehand as well. Illustrator's tools are rudimentary compared to an image editor's (see the sidebar, "Image Processing in Illustrator," at the end of this chapter).

6.40 It's best not to scale your images within Illustrator. Use an image editor instead.

- For UI design, use images in the RGB color space, which will help ensure good color fidelity and accuracy when the final art ends up in development. CMYK images will be larger and the color may not be ideal since a fewer number of colors can be displayed in this color space.

- Save your image files in PSD or TIFF before importing. You can import JPGs and GIFs, but if you try to export from Illustrator, you'll end up double-compressing them. Linking your files will save this step, as you can just use the original file as an asset in the final system.

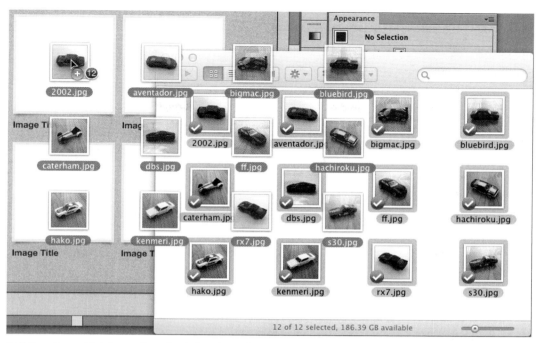

6.41 Dragging multiple images from the desktop into a document

Importing Images

To get images into Illustrator, you can either copy and paste from an image editor like Photoshop, drag them from the desktop into an Illustrator window, or import them using the Place command. With the photo frames you created earlier, you'll have the opportunity to add several images into the Wheelr layout. You can download several images of toy cars from www.peachpit.com/UIwithAI/ch6/cars.zip. To import multiple files at once, follow these steps:

1. Unzip the **cars.zip** file and open the folder.

   This folder contains the 12 images you'll need to import into Illustrator for the layout.

2. Select all 12 files and drag them into the wheelr.ai window (**6.41**).

   Dragging images automatically links them to the original file. If you wish to embed any of them at this point, select the desired images and click the Embed button in the Control panel. Using File > Place allows you to specify linking or embedding at import.

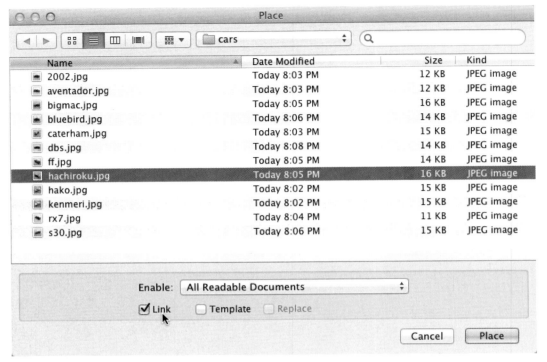

6.42 When using the File > Place command, you can choose whether to link the image.

To import one file at a time:

1. Choose File > Place and navigate to the folder of images.

2. Select the file to import, choose whether to link the file (**6.42**), and then click Place.

    Importing images one at a time allows you the option to link or embed. The next time you import, Illustrator remembers the previous setting so you don't have to specify every time.

When an image is selected, additional options are available in the Control panel (**6.43**). Besides showing the color space and image resolution, you can embed it, edit it in an image editor, and even perform an image trace function. Furthermore, the filename appears as a link that displays a menu of useful commands (**6.44**).

Once you have all the car images in Illustrator, you can use the tools to move them, transform them, and select them for adding effects. Go ahead and move each of the 12 cars into position inside the photo frames (**6.45**).

6.43 Image options in the Control panel

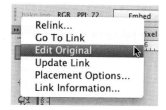

6.44 Image commands from the file link

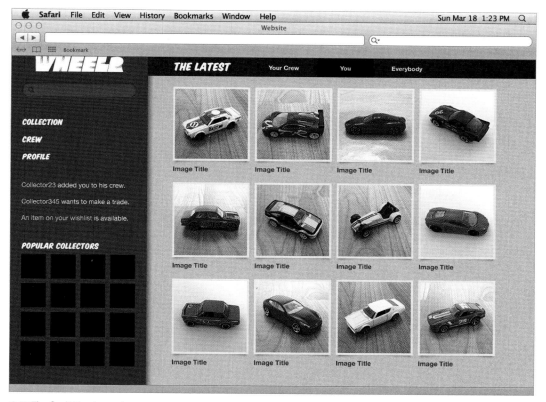

6.45 The final Wheelr mockup

Image Processing in Illustrator

Illustrator does provide a couple of basic image processing features to use in a pinch. These features are intended for use on vector objects, but they do work on images as well. You can find these tools in the Edit > Edit Colors menu (**6.46**).

6.47 Click the Embed button to embed an image in Illustrator.

6.46 Edit Colors features for image processing

These features work only on embedded images. To embed an image, select it and click the Embed button in the Control panel (**6.47**). When using the Saturate color filter, you'll get an error message as you try to apply the filter, but you can just click OK to dismiss it (**6.48**).

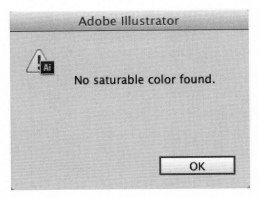

6.48 Dismiss this error message when you see it. The filter still works.

Conclusion

And with that, the Wheelr mockup is complete. This was an exercise designed to get you familiar with the concepts and tools and hopefully served to inspire you to go even further. Take some time to play around with the layout, colors, textures, and content to discover even more possibilities. This really is only the beginning of what you can do with UI design in Illustrator.

The next chapter will teach you how you can integrate Illustrator into your workflow to help you be more efficient without stifling your creativity.

TABLE 6.1 Keyboard Shortcuts in This Chapter

	MAC	PC
Undo	⌘Z	Ctrl+Z
Deselect	⌘⇧A	Ctrl+Shift+A
Bring to Front	⌘⇧]	Ctrl+Shift+]
Send to Back	⌘⇧[	Ctrl+Shift+[
Cut	⌘X	Ctrl+X
Paste	⌘V	Ctrl+V

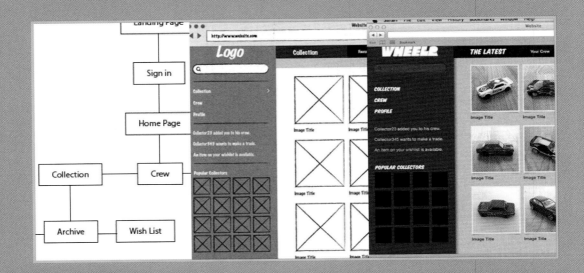

7

WORKING SMARTER

Chapter Overview

So far, you've learned how Illustrator's tools work and how to use them to create a single mockup. This final chapter will explain how you can use Illustrator's tools and techniques to work smarter as you begin to use it for larger projects. This chapter focuses on ways you can use Illustrator to create a fast and efficient workflow:

- Planning UI design

- Communicating your design intentions

- Creating a style library

- Getting your work out of Illustrator

UI Design Planning

UI design isn't easy. There are a lot of steps to take when creating a system or application. It's pretty difficult to just sit down and start designing a user interface without putting some thought into it first. Sure, as a creative person, you might sit down and test a few visual ideas as they pop into your head. There's nothing wrong with taking advantage of a little inspiration. But to develop a successful design, you'll want plan the design so that you understand the scope of what you need to create.

UI design is just one piece of a process for user experience design. There are many methods to planning the user experience of a project. That subject falls outside the scope of this book; in fact, there are shelves of books dedicated to the topic. However, Illustrator is extremely useful for this part of the process. From information architecture to interaction design to visual design, you can efficiently use one tool for the job so that you don't have to start all over again as you move through the process.

While you can certainly utilize Illustrator's comprehensive text-editing features for any upfront documentation, I focus on the visual deliverables of the planning process in this section.

User Experience Resources

Here is a list of some great books on UX and interaction design that helped me learn the ropes:

- *Simple and Usable Web, Mobile, and Interaction Design*, Giles Colborne (New Riders)

- *The Elements of User Experience: User-Centered Design for the Web*, Jesse James Garrett (New Riders)

- *Designing the Obvious: A Common Sense Approach to Web & Mobile Application Design*, Robert Hoekman (Pearson Education/Voices that Matter)

- *Designing the Moment: Web Interface Design Concepts in Action*, Robert Hoekman (New Riders)

- *Don't Make Me Think: A Common Sense Approach to Web Usability*, Steve Krug (New Riders)

- *The Design of Everyday Things*, Donald A. Norman (Basic Books)

- *Designing for Interaction: Creating Smart Applications and Clever Devices*, Dan Saffer (New Riders)

- *Designing Interfaces: Patterns for Effective Interaction Design*, Jenifer Tidwell (O'Reilly)

Creating a Site Map

One of the beginning steps in the process of creating a good user experience is that of information architecture. The Information Architecture Institute (www.iainstitute.org) defines information architecture as "the art and science of organizing and labeling websites, intranets, online communities and software to support usability." Basically, the task of the information architect is to provide a means of organizing content with the proper context so that the user can easily find the right information.

One of the tools you'll use to do this is a site map. This is a diagram of the site structure used as a map of all the content on the site. While there are other tools dedicated to the task of building site maps, simple site maps can be created right inside Illustrator. In fact, you can include your site map in the same doc you use for the rest of the project, making it convenient to refer to while designing.

Before you create the site map, you should have a concrete plan for the content contained in the application. You'll then organize that content into logical sections. You can use plain rectangles, ellipses, or other shapes to represent the pages in the app, or you can add a little style to the diagram (**7.1**). In this exercise, you'll learn how to use graphic styles to speed up the creation of a simple site map.

1. Choose File > New (⌘N/Ctrl+N) to create a new document. Select the Web profile and choose the 1024x768 artboard size. Then click OK.

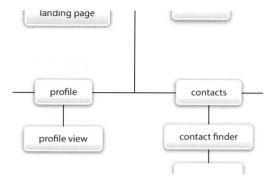

7.1 A site map with style

2. Choose View > Smart Guides (⌘U/Ctrl+U) to turn on Smart Guides. If there is already a check mark next to the menu item (**7.2**), you can skip this step.

Using Smart Guides will help you to keep your site map elements lined up neatly and will aid in the creation of connector lines.

3. Select the Type tool  (T) and click once to create a point type object, and then type *Landing Page* on the artboard.

4. In the Control panel at the top of the screen, select the Align Center button (**7.3**) to change the text alignment.

Creating a Dynamic Page Symbol

Now that you have the first page of the application represented with text, you'll add a page symbol. A site map uses objects called *symbols* (not to be confused with an Illustrator symbol) to represent a page, group of pages, or bits of programming logic. What makes it dynamic is that the element itself will resize based on the text inside of it. You'll save this element as a graphic style that can be used for the rest of the site map.

1. Click the text with the Selection tool ▶ (V) to select it. Remove its fill by choosing the None swatch in the Swatches panel (**7.4**).

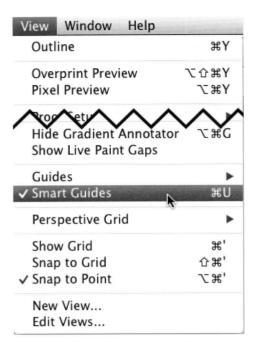

7.2 Smart Guides can be toggled in the View menu.

7.3 The Align Center button

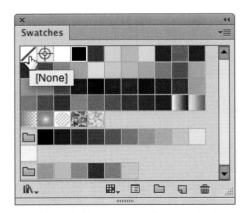

7.4 Clicking the None swatch will remove the fill from the text.

2. In the Appearance panel, click the Add New Fill button 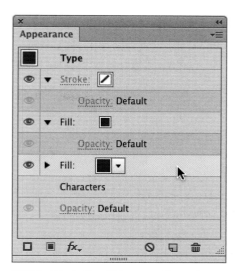 at the bottom of the panel twice to add two new fills to the appearance stack.

   The top fill in this stack will provide the color for the text, while the bottom one will be converted to a rectangle.

3. Click the bottom fill in the appearance stack (7.5) and choose Effect > Convert to Shape > Rectangle.

4. In the Shape Options dialog box, choose Relative for the size, and enter 18 px and 9 px in the Extra Width and Extra Height fields, respectively (7.6). Then click OK.

   Choosing Relative will allow the rectangle to automatically resize to fit any text entered in the page icon. This is the key element of this exercise.

7.5 Select the bottom fill to convert it to a shape.

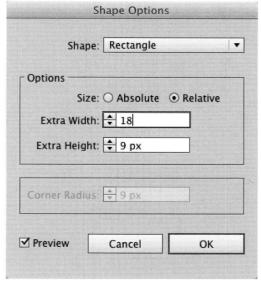

7.6 Choosing the Relative size option allows you to specify how much space to add around the text.

5. With the bottom fill still selected, change the color to white from the fill's Color pop-up (**7.7**).

6. Click the Stroke layer in the Appearance panel. Change the stroke to 1 px, and then choose Effect > Convert to Shape > Rectangle. Use the same settings as in step 4.

7. Choose New Graphic Style from the Graphic Style panel menu (Window > Graphic Styles) and name the new style *Page*.

You now have a dynamic page symbol (**7.8**) to use throughout the site map. It is dynamic in that the box will automatically resize to fit any text within it.

TIP You can change the stroke units to pixels in the Preferences dialog box. You can access this setting directly by using the keyboard shortcut ⌘, (comma)/Ctrl+, (comma).

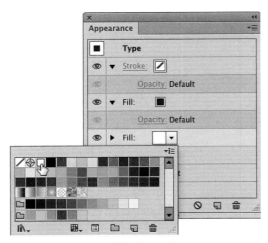

7.7 Change the bottom fill color to white.

Landing Page

7.8 This page indicator will resize automatically as new text is entered.

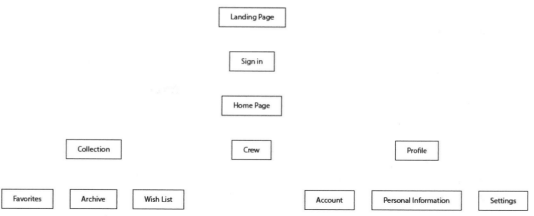

7.9 The site map before connector lines are added

Organize Pages

Once you have the page indicator to represent a page in the application, you can fill out the rest of the map to match **7.9**. All you need to do is type the name of each page of the site, apply the graphic style you created in the previous section, and then arrange each indicator to match the desired structure. Use the alignment tools (covered at the beginning of Chapter 4) to align and space them perfectly. When you have finished, use the Line Segment tool ✎ (\) to draw connector lines to show the relationships between each page.

1. Select the Line Segment tool (\).

2. Hover your mouse near the bottom-center of the Landing Page icon. The Smart Guides will highlight when you have reached the center point of the box (**7.10**).

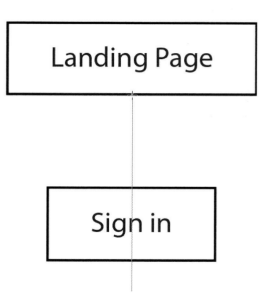

7.10 Smart Guides show the center of the nearest object.

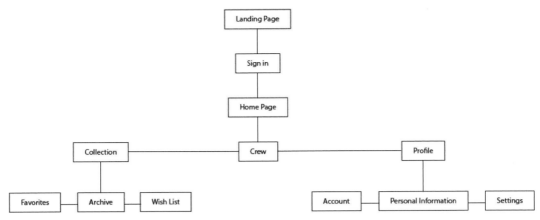

7.12 The finished site map

3. Click and drag to create the segment. The Smart Guide will constrain the segment to the vertical axis and automatically snap to the next symbol (**7.11**).

4. Repeat the steps to create all the connector lines (**7.12**).

Creating a site map is as simple as that. As you edit the text within the page symbols, the box grows or shrinks to fit automatically. You can change the Page graphic style to edit the design at any time.

NOTE See Chapter 5 to learn how to create and edit graphic styles.

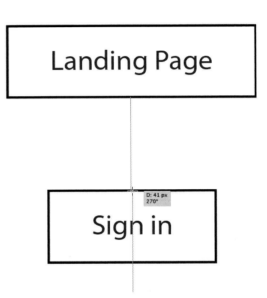

7.11 The Smart Guide constrains the new line segment and shows its distance and angle.

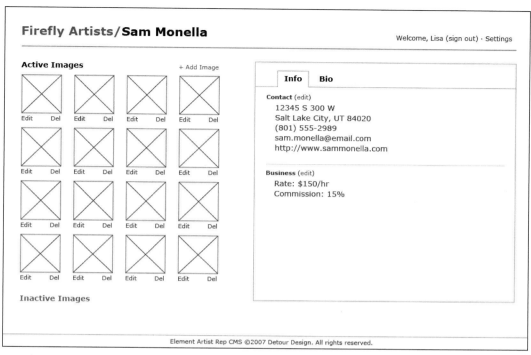

7.13 The "Plain Jane" wireframe style

Creating Wireframes

Another step in the user experience design process is the creation of wireframes. Wireframing takes the information learned from content strategy, information architecture, user research, and functional analysis to begin the process of structuring a design. Wireframes are used to determine layout, feature placement, and design patterns, and are usually a rough representation of the final product. They are typically devoid of style so as to not distract from making sure that the structure and content are correct.

Several different wireframe styles are commonly used today. I have dubbed these the plain jane (**7.13**), gray box (**7.14**), and sketch styles (**7.15**).

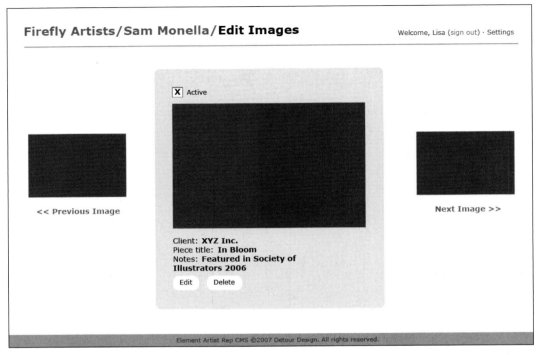

7.14 The "Gray Box" wireframe style

While the styles themselves are fairly different, there are some conventions I like to follow when creating wireframe elements in Illustrator:

- **Don't worry about typography, but do worry about visual hierarchy.** Use only one typeface while wireframing, but do use different sizes. In fact, the closer you can get to the sizes to be used in the final design, the less fiddling you'll have to do when converting your wireframes to final artwork.

- **Use photo indication, not actual photos.** This keeps your file light and fast. The rough representation also keeps the focus on the content and structure of the page, rather than on the photography.

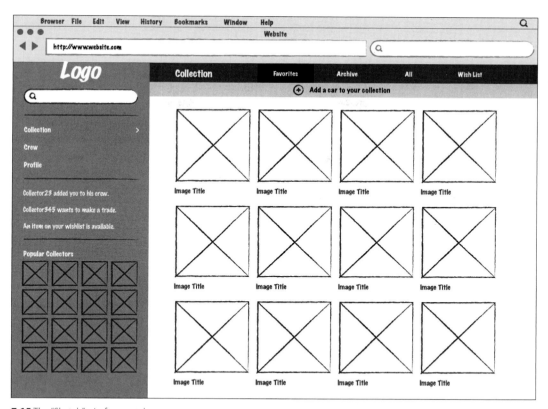

7.15 The "Sketch" wireframe style

- **Don't worry too much about the pixel grid.** You can always tighten up the layout once you get to the final mockup stage.

- **Use graphic styles and symbols in your wireframes.** This is helpful for two reasons. First, if you create symbols and graphic styles of your wireframe elements, you won't have to recreate them every time you start a new project. Second, with symbols, you can use sublayers (layers within layers) to keep both the wireframe element and the final element in the same symbol.

Communicate Your Design Intentions

If you work with a team to create software, you'll learn that communicating with your team about how your design works will make developing the application much smoother. As a designer, you probably have a lot of this information in your head. However, if you don't communicate that information to your developers, there will be a lot of questions down the road. What follows are a few different methods for communicating your design intentions.

Visualizing Interactions with Storyboards

As you design a user interface, it's important to think about how the user will interact with the features you are creating. It's even more important to let your development team know how those interactions work as they develop those features. While sitting with your team and explaining your ideas to them in detail might work, it's better to clearly communicate the ideas to them in a way that they can visualize what you need.

If you are adept at creating clickable prototypes, you can probably skip this section, because I feel that's the best way to show how features and interactions are designed to work. But if that option is outside your skill set or job description, you'll need a way to communicate your intent. Storyboards are a great way to show step-by-step how a feature is designed to work.

Creating low-fidelity storyboards at the beginning is a quick way to get your ideas out of your head to see whether they work the way you envision them. This method uses sketches in frames to represent each step of the interaction. You'll use this method to sketch out how adding a car to your collection in Wheelr might work.

Since this is primarily a sketching exercise, why include it here? You can use Illustrator to create the template for your storyboards and then bring your sketches back into Illustrator for archiving. To complete this exercise, I created a storyboard template for you to use. To download this template, go to www.peachpit.com/UIwithAI/ch7/storyboard.ai.

As you open this file, you'll see that it has storyboards for a browser, tablet, and smartphone, each on a separate layer. To use a certain storyboard, show its layer and hide the others. For this exercise, you'll use the browser layer.

> **NOTE** In case you jumped into the book at this point, Wheelr is an example web application that was mocked up in Chapters 4, 5, and 6.

> **NOTE** You can find out more about how to work with layers in Chapter 5.

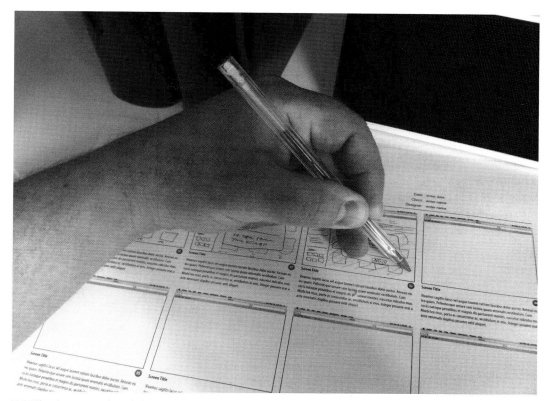

7.16 Sketch your storyboard ideas on the template.

1. Print the storyboard file and use as many panels as you need to sketch out the interaction (**7.16**).

2. There are many ways to get your sketches into Illustrator. One way is to use the camera on your phone to capture the sketches and send them to your desktop via email or a cloud service. You can also use a scanner to capture the images.

3. Using your preferred photo editor, crop each image to the size of the sketch, eliminating any of the printed matter.

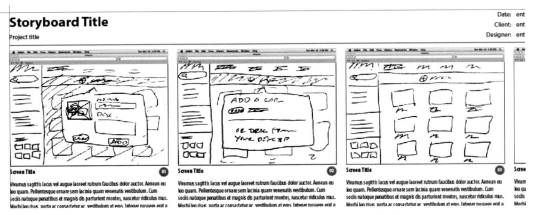

Storyboard Title
Project title

Date: ent
Client: ent
Designer: ent

Screen Title   01

Vivamus sagittis lacus vel augue laoreet rutrum faucibus dolor auctor. Aenean eu leo quam. Pellentesque ornare sem lacinia quam venenatis vestibulum. Cum sociis natoque penatibus et magnis dis parturient montes, nascetur ridiculus mus. Morbi leo risus, porta ac consectetur ac, vestibulum at eros. Integer posuere erat a

Screen Title   02

Vivamus sagittis lacus vel augue laoreet rutrum faucibus dolor auctor. Aenean eu leo quam. Pellentesque ornare sem lacinia quam venenatis vestibulum. Cum sociis natoque penatibus et magnis dis parturient montes, nascetur ridiculus mus. Morbi leo risus, porta ac consectetur ac, vestibulum at eros. Integer posuere erat a

Screen Title   03

Vivamus sagittis lacus vel augue laoreet rutrum faucibus dolor auctor. Aenean eu leo quam. Pellentesque ornare sem lacinia quam venenatis vestibulum. Cum sociis natoque penatibus et magnis dis parturient montes, nascetur ridiculus mus. Morbi leo risus, porta ac consectetur ac, vestibulum at eros. Integer posuere erat a

7.17 Scan, edit, and place your sketches in the digital storyboard for presentation and archival purposes.

4. Back in Illustrator, choose File > Place for each image and use the Scale tool ⬚ (S) or the Free Transform tool ⬚ (E) to size and position each sketch within its respective panel (**7.17**).

5. Press ⌘⇧S/Ctrl+Shift+S to save your storyboard to a new file.

Once you have the interactions worked out, you can create the high-fidelity storyboards in Illustrator using wireframes.

Set Up the Storyboard

To document how the interaction works, you'll use multiple artboards, one for each state. To complete this exercise, download and open the wireframe file at www.peachpit.com/UIwithAI/ch7/add-car.ai. This file has the first artboard in the interaction sequence already completed. It also contains all the symbols and graphic styles necessary to build the sequence.

1. Using the Artboards panel, duplicate the current artboard by dragging it to the New Artboard icon 🗔 at the bottom of the panel (**7.18**).

2. Double-click the artboard name in the panel and rename the artboard *add car popover*.

NOTE I used the font Marker Felt for the wireframe. If you don't have this font, you'll get a warning message when you open the file. Click Open to ignore this warning. You can use any informal-looking font from your font list instead.

Create the Popover Interaction

Now, you'll create the first interaction state in this sequence, which is a popover for adding a new car image to the collection:

1. Create a new layer in the Layers panel (Window > Layers). Double-click the name and rename it *add car popover*.

2. Select the new layer you just created and drag it above the Content layer (**7.19**).

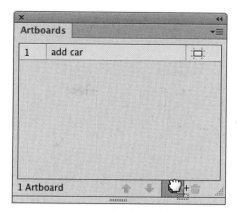

7.18 Drag the artboard to the New Artboard icon to duplicate it.

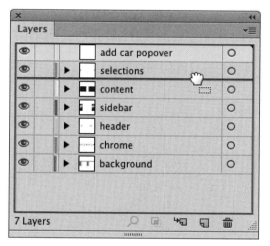

7.19 Drag layers to rearrange their stacking order.

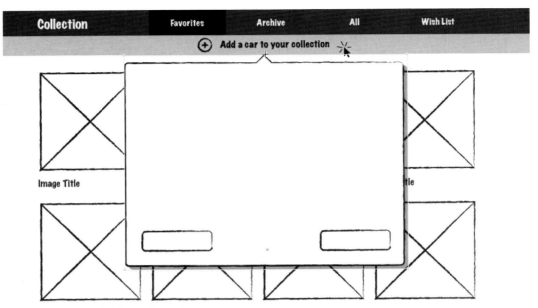

7.20 The popover symbol dragged into place

3. From the Symbols panel (Window > Symbols), drag the popover symbol onto the artboard (**7.20**).

4. With the Type tool (T), click once in the popover and type *Add a Car to Your Collection* (**7.21**). Format the type to your liking and then press Escape to leave text-editing mode.

7.21 Adding a title to the popover

5. Click within the left button on the pop-over and type *Cancel*. Press Escape and then click within the bounds of the pop-over's right button and type *Add* (**7.22**).

6. With the Rectangle tool 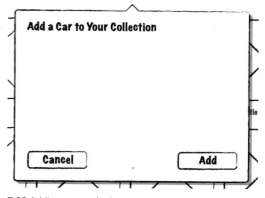 (M), click in the popover and create a 355 px wide by 180 px tall rectangle (**7.23**). This will be the drop zone for images to be uploaded.

7. With the Brushes panel (Window > Brushes), click the Charcoal – Pencil brush to add a sketchy outline to the rectangle (**7.24**).

7.22 Adding text to the buttons

7.23 Adding the drop zone rectangle

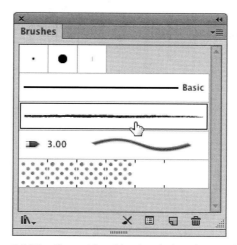

7.24 The Charcoal-Pencil brush is the key element of the sketchy wireframe style.

8. To give the rectangle a fill, double-click the Fill indicator in the Tools panel and type *e2e2e2* in the hexadecimal color field (**7.25**).

9. Select the Type tool (T) again, click once in the rectangle, and type *Drag files here from the desktop* (**7.26**).

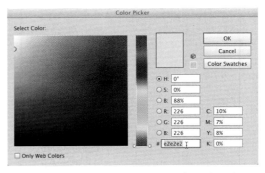

7.25 Recoloring the drop zone rectangle from the Color Picker

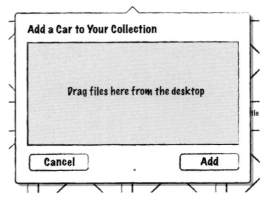

7.26 The instruction text for the drop zone

Create the Next State

Now you'll duplicate the current artboard to create the third state. This state will show what it looks like once a file has been dragged in from the desktop and the user is about to click the Add button.

1. Using the Artboards panel, duplicate the add car popover artboard by dragging it to the New Artboard icon ⬚ at the bottom of the panel.

2. Double-click the new artboard name in the panel and rename the artboard *drag image to add*.

3. Delete the "Drag files…" text. From the Symbols panel (Window > Symbols), drag the cursor click, thumbnail, text field, horizontal rule, and icon delete symbols into the popover. Arrange them as shown in **7.27**.

4. Select the Type tool (T) and click just above the text field. Type *Image Title*. Press Escape and then click in the text field and type *Treasure Hunts 240Z* (**7.28**).

5. Drag the cursor click symbol onto the Add button to make it look like it's being clicked (**7.29**).

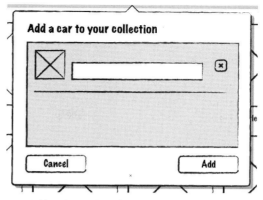

7.27 Adding the symbols for the dropped art

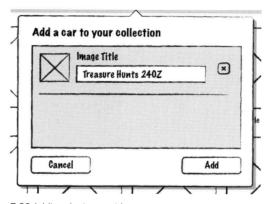

7.28 Adding the image title text

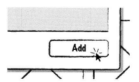

7.29 Using a symbol to indicate a click

Create the Final State

The final state of this interaction will show the page with the new image added. You'll put a label on the new image to give the user feedback as to which one was just added.

1. Using the Artboards panel, duplicate the *drag image to add* artboard by dragging it to the New Artboard icon ⬚ at the bottom of the panel.

2. Double-click the new artboard name in the panel and rename the artboard to *image added*.

3. Delete the popover from this artboard. Click the first Image Title label (**7.30**) and choose Object > Expand Appearance.

   Expanding an appearance removes any live effects from an object. Because this text used the Transform effect to repeat it across and down, any change made to the text would be repeated in all the copies. To show the user feedback for an added image, you'll want to break that link so you only change the filename of the first title.

4. Select the Type tool (T) and triple-click the first Image Title. Triple-clicking will engage type-editing mode and select the text simultaneously. Type *Treasure Hunts 240Z* (**7.31**).

   As the final step, you'll add a snipe symbol to the corner of the image to show that it is new.

5. From the Symbols panel, drag the snipe symbol onto the artboard. Position it at the corner of the first image (**7.32**).

6. Press ⌘S/Ctrl+S to save your work.

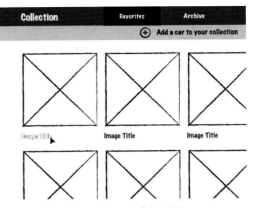

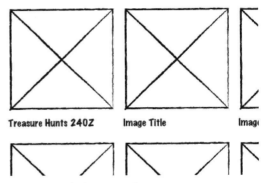

7.30 Expanding the appearance of the label

7.31 Naming the "new image"

7.32 Adding the corner snipe

Adding Notes

Another way to communicate your design intentions is by adding notes to your mock-ups. Because of the editable nature of artboards, you can include notes on the wireframe or mockup itself in a very simple way.

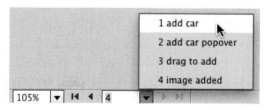

7.33 Using the artboard navigator to switch artboards

1. Using the storyboard wireframes you created in the last section, navigate to the *add car* artboard by selecting it in the artboard navigator at the bottom of the document window (**7.33**).

2. Click the Artboard tool ⊡ (Shift-O) and drag the bottom of the artboard to resize it slightly (**7.34**).

3. Select the Type tool (T) and drag to create an area type box in the empty space below the design. You can type notes in this space relating to the design of the screen (**7.35**).

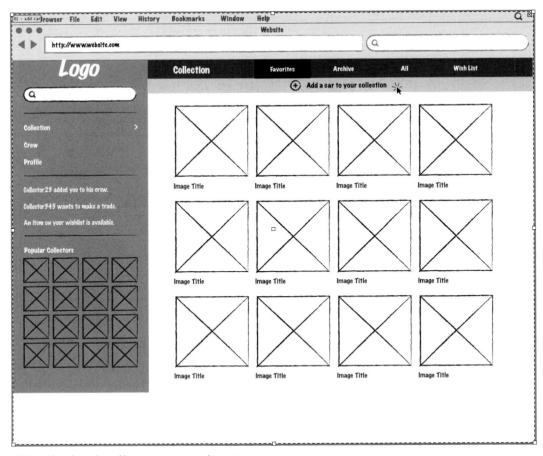

7.34 Making the artboard larger to accommodate notes

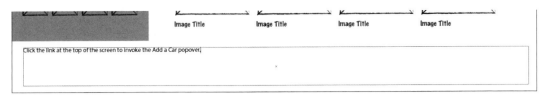

7.35 Adding notes to the wireframe

Another way to leave notes on your design is with a virtual sticky note. Since Illustrator doesn't have a built-in annotation tool, you can create your own virtual sticky note and save it as a scalable symbol that can be reused as often as you need. Here's how to create it:

1. Using the storyboard wireframes again, select the Rectangle tool (M) and click to create a 300 px wide by 300 px tall rectangle. Give the rectangle a white fill.

2. In the Layers panel, move the rectangle to the content layer by dragging the colored square to the appropriate layer (**7.36**).

3. With the rectangle still selected, press F8 to create a new symbol. In the dialog box, type *Sticky Note* as the name and select the 9-slice scaling option. Deselect the Align to Pixel Grid option. Click OK (**7.37**).

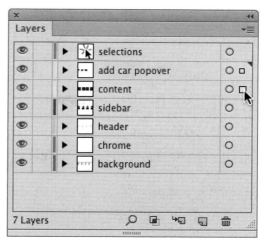

7.36 Drag the color square to move objects between layers.

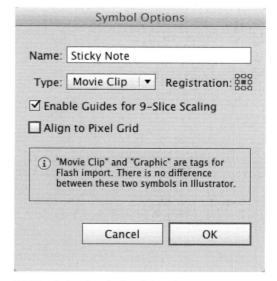

7.37 Symbol settings for the sticky note

Adding Color

1. Double-click the symbol in the Symbols panel to enter isolation mode.

   The first thing you'll need to do is add color to the rectangle. Then you'll add some stylistic touches to make it look more realistic.

2. Select the rectangle and press the > (greater than symbol) key to add a gradient. In the Gradient panel (Window > Gradient), double-click the first color stop, change the color mode to RGB in the panel menu, and enter *d3d540* in the hexadecimal color field (**7.38**).

3. Double-click the second color stop and repeat step 2, except enter *f3f560* in the hex color field.

4. Change the angle in the Angle field (**7.39**) to 90 degrees.

Adding Style

Now you'll add some live effects with the Appearance panel to give the sticky note a more realistic look.

1. With the rectangle selected, click the Fill layer in the Appearance panel (Window > Appearance).

2. Choose Effect > Distort & Transform > Tweak. In the dialog box, select the Absolute radio button and set both the Horizontal and Vertical amounts to 3 px. In the Modify section, select only the Anchor Points and 'In' Control Points options (**7.40**). Click OK.

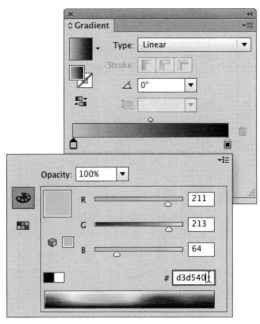

7.38 Setting the color for the first color stop

7.39 Adjusting the gradient angle

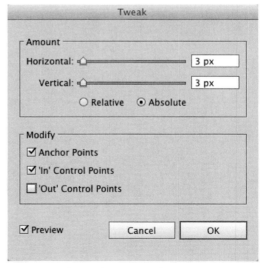

7.40 Setting the Tweak parameters for the sticky note

You should end up with a rectangle that is slightly tweaked (**7.41**). This looks more realistic than a perfect square.

3. In the Appearance panel, add another Fill layer by clicking Add New Fill button 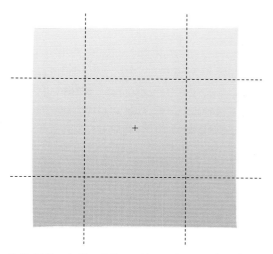 at the bottom of the panel. Color this fill black by clicking the swatch pop-up and choosing the black swatch (**7.42**).

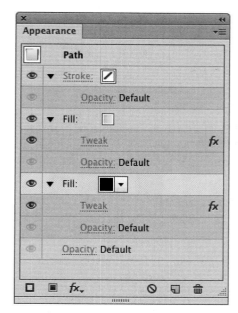

7.41 Adding the Tweak filter adds a realistic touch to the sticky note.

7.42 Coloring the bottom fill black

4. Choose Effect > Distort & Transform > Transform. Select the Preview option and experiment with the settings until it looks right to your eye (**7.43**). Click OK.

5. Change the Opacity of the bottom fill to 50% and choose Multiply from the blend mode pop-up (**7.44**).

NOTE I can't be more specific about what settings to use for this particular effect because it is totally random and different every time. Experiment with the Scale and Move settings until the shadow looks realistic to your eye.

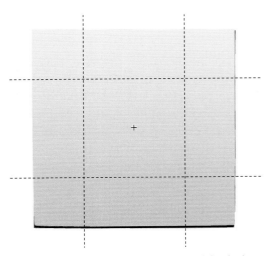

7.43 Adjust the Transform effect settings until the shadow looks right.

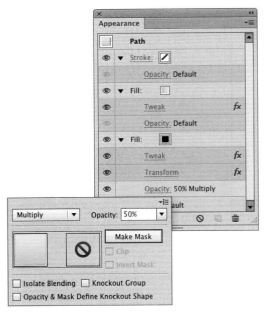

7.44 Adjusting transparency settings on the bottom fill

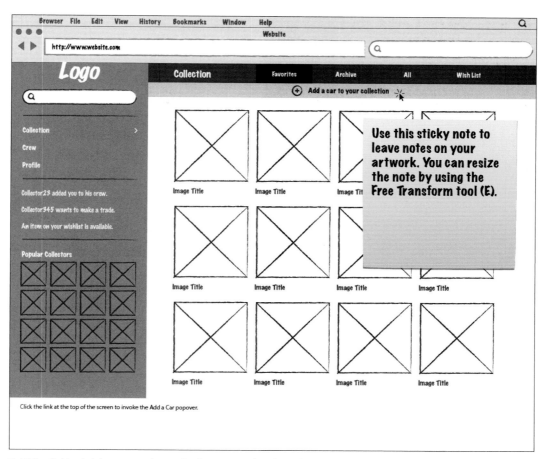

Use this sticky note to leave notes on your artwork. You can resize the note by using the Free Transform tool (E).

7.45 The finished sticky note can be used to leave notes directly on the artwork.

6. Press Escape to leave isolation mode.

    You now have a resizable Sticky Note symbol that you can use to leave annotations directly on your document (**7.45**). This is especially helpful if you work with others that will access your Illustrator file. You could create a different color sticky note for each person that will comment on the file.

NOTE Why not just use the Drop Shadow effect? When striving for this type of look, canned effects are less customizable and therefore less realistic.

Style Libraries

As you begin to get comfortable doing UI design with Illustrator, you'll start to use it for larger projects. It's helpful to create a style guide for a large project, as it provides an easy way to access, document, and share styles with your teams. One of the best ways to do this is to create a file that contains all of your app's graphic elements with each of their corresponding states. One of the benefits of creating this type of guide is that it helps you achieve consistency in your design.

You can start small and fill in the guide as you flesh out the design. Once you have every element completed, Illustrator allows you to save portable libraries for color schemes, symbols, and graphic styles, as well as character and paragraph styles. You can then package all of these into a template you can use when you begin a new project.

The next few sections walk you through how to do this.

NOTE The inspiration for this style guide comes from Yaron Schoen, who created one for a site called Kontain. You can see what his style guide looked like by going to http://d.pr/WYmp.

Create Color Schemes

There are several ways to create compelling color schemes in Illustrator. If you are an expert at choosing coordinating colors, you can do it the manual way by creating some squares on the artboard and mixing colors until you have something you like. But if you're color-challenged, Illustrator can help you out with a couple of unique tools.

Color Guide

The first of these tools is the Color Guide panel (Window > Color Guide). This panel is a robust color inspiration tool that allows you to find and create color schemes based on harmony rules and preset swatch libraries (**7.46**). When I say robust, I mean robust. So much, in fact, that I will only be able to cover a small portion of what this panel can do. Let's try it out to create a new color scheme:

1. Open a new document (⌘N/Ctrl+N) and then open the Color Guide panel by choosing Window > Color Guide.

2. Select the Rectangle tool (M) and draw any size rectangle on the artboard. Give it a fill by choosing any color from the Swatches panel (Window > Swatches). This will allow you experiment with colors and see the results.

3. Select the rectangle and then click a color variation in the Color Guide panel (**7.47**).

   The rectangle you created will be filled with the color you clicked. Now it's time to have some fun.

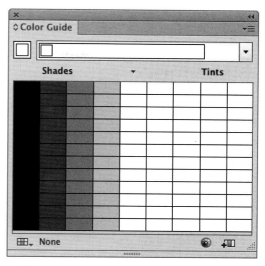

7.46 The Color Guide panel

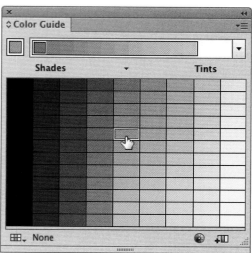

7.47 Coloring the rectangle with a variation swatch

4. In the Color Guide panel, click the Base Color button (**7.48**) to set this new color as the base color for the color scheme.

   You'll notice that the color variations all change in relation to the new base color.

5. Click the Harmony Rules menu and select a harmony rule. (I chose the Complementary 2 rule in **7.49**.)

7.48 Click the Base Color button to set a new base color for the scheme.

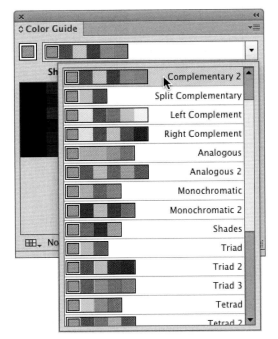

7.49 Choosing a harmony rule

Now you're looking at shades and tints of the active color set in the color variation pane (**7.50**). You can also view variations based on Warm/Cool colors or Vivid/Muted colors by selecting the appropriate set from the panel menu. For now, go ahead and stick with tints and shades.

6. You can select color variations based on a preset swatch library as well. Click the Swatch Library button 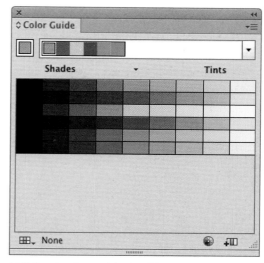 and choose Nature > Landscape.

    The variations adjust again, this time creating a nice blend of cool and warm colors. You can save these colors as a group of swatches for use in a project.

7. To save the color group, click the Save Color Group to Swatch panel button ▣ at the bottom of the Color Guide panel.

    Open the Swatch panel (Window > Swatches) to see that Illustrator has created a group of swatches for you (**7.51**). You can rename this color group by double-clicking the folder icon and naming it in the dialog box that appears.

You just created your first color scheme. When you have some time, play around with the Color Guide panel and see what you can come up with on your own. You'll find that it can help immensely as a tool for color inspiration.

7.50 Showing tints and shades of the active colors

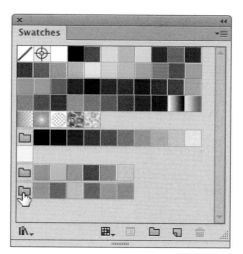

7.51 Color groups are indicated with a folder icon.

Kuler

Another tool for color inspiration is Adobe's own Kuler plug-in. Adobe released Kuler several years ago as a website where a large community of users create, save, and share color themes. It was such a useful tool that Adobe integrated it as a plug-in panel within Illustrator. The panel contains user-created themes with search and filtering functions to help you find the colors you're looking for. To open the Kuler panel, choose Window > Extensions > Kuler.

By default, the panel shows the top 10 most popular themes of all time (**7.52**). You can page through these themes with the arrows at the top of the panel. To change the sorting, select the desired criteria from the pop-up menus. Hovering over a theme shows metadata and a star rating. To add the theme as a color group to the Swatches panel, click the "Add selected theme to Swatches panel" button ▦ at the bottom of the Kuler panel. Finally, you can upload your own color schemes to Kuler by selecting a scheme in your Swatches panel and clicking the "Upload from Swatch Panel to Kuler community" ▦ button at the bottom of the Kuler panel. Your default web browser will launch and go to http://kuler.adobe.com. You'll need to sign in with your Adobe ID before you can save your theme

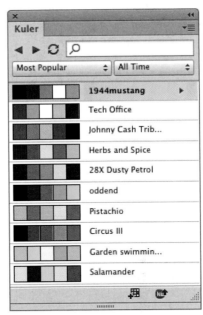

7.52 The Kuler panel

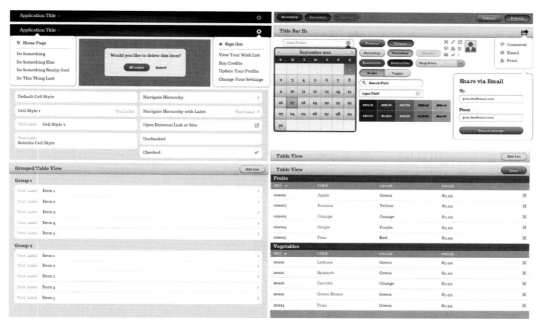

7.53 A sample style guide

Portable Colors, Symbols, and Styles

With a style guide in place, you can use your colors, symbols, and styles in other documents without having to recreate them from scratch. You can also save your color swatches to be used in other applications that support the Adobe Swatch Exchange (.ase) file format for import. To see how this works, download the example style guide mentioned earlier from www.peachpit.com/UIwithAI/ch7/style-guide.ai. This file contains a couple of color groups, a collection of symbols, and graphic, character, and paragraph styles (**7.53**).

NOTE To get the most out of this style guide, go to www.fontsquirrel.com and download Trocchi, a free web font.

Open the Swatches panel (Window > Swatches) to find that there are three color groups included. To save these color groups for use in another document, perform the following steps:

1. From the Swatches panel menu, choose Save Swatch Library as AI. In the Save As dialog box, navigate to your desired folder; give the file a memorable name and then click Save.

2. To save the color groups for use in InDesign or Photoshop, choose Save Swatch Library as ASE from the panel menu. The file will be saved in a format that you can load into one of those applications.

Templates

Once you have a style guide completed, all your graphic, character, and paragraph styles created, and a symbol library finished, you can create a template file that can be used to create new documents. A new document created from a template opens with all your settings in place, ready for you to begin designing. You can build as many templates as necessary to fit the needs of your project. Using templates can save tons of time.

To create a template based on the style guide from the previous sections, complete the following steps:

1. Create a new document (⌘N/Ctrl+N). In the New Document dialog box, be sure to set the doc up with settings that you'll need when you use the template to create a new project file.

   This means that your profile, number of artboards, artboard dimensions, and advanced settings all get saved with the template. Don't worry, though, you can change it later by overwriting the old template file with a new one.

2. Once you have all your document settings as you like, click OK to create the new file.

   Now it's time to load all your symbols, colors, and styles. If you haven't downloaded the style guide file, go to www.peachpit.com/UIwitrhAI/ch7/style-guide.ai to grab it.

Load Symbols

First, you'll need to load your symbols. Before you do that, though, open the Symbols panel (Window > Symbols) and choose Select All Unused from the panel menu. Click the Delete Symbol button 🗑 at the bottom of the panel. This removes all the default symbols that ship with Illustrator, giving you a clean slate from which to start. You'll do the same with graphic styles and swatches.

1. Click the Symbol Libraries Menu button 📚 and choose Other Library from the menu. Navigate to where you saved the style_guide.ai file and click Open.

   A new Symbols panel opens containing the symbols from the style guide.

2. Click the first symbol and then Shift-click the last one to select all. Drag all the symbols into the default Symbols panel (**7.54**).

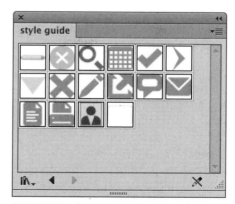

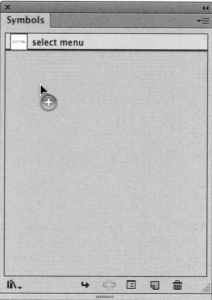

7.54 Adding symbols from one file into another

Load Graphic Styles

Second, you'll load your graphic styles. To clear out the defaults, open the Graphic Styles panel (Window > Graphic Styles) and choose Select All Unused from the panel menu. Click the Delete Graphic Style button 🗑 to remove them.

1. Click the Graphic Style Libraries Menu button 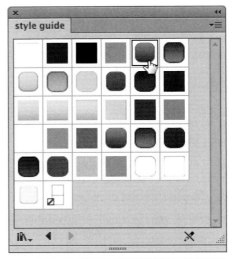 and choose Other Library from the menu. Again, navigate to the style_guide.ai file and click Open.

   A new Graphic Styles panel opens, containing the styles from that file.

2. Click the first style and Shift-click the last to select all. Drag these styles into the default Graphic Styles panel (**7.55**).

7.55 Adding styles into the new document.

Load Color Swatches and Groups

Third, you'll add your colors. Clear out the defaults by opening the Swatches panel (Window > Swatches) and following the steps as before. If any remain, select the stubborn ones and click the Delete Swatch button 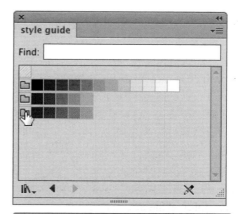.

1. Click the Swatch Libraries Menu button ▮▾ and choose Other Library from the menu. Navigate to the style_guide.ai file and click Open.

    A new Swatches panel will open containing the swatches from that file.

2. Click the folder icon at the front of each color group and drag them to the default Swatches panel (**7.56**).

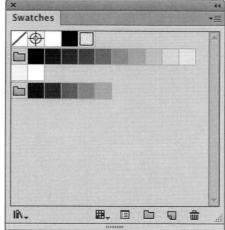

7.56 Click and drag the folder icons to add color groups to the new file.

Load Character and Paragraph Styles

Finally, you'll add your text styles. This is the easiest of the bunch, because there aren't any defaults to remove and you can add all styles with a click.

1. From the Window menu, open either the Character Styles (Window > Type > Character Styles) or Paragraph Styles (Window > Type> Paragraph Styles) panel (it doesn't matter which).

2. From the panel menu, choose Load All Styles (**7.57**). Then navigate to the style guide file to load the styles.

    This option loads both character and paragraph styles in one shot (**7.58**).

Save the Template

The last step is to save the template file by doing the following:

1. Choose File > Save as Template.

2. Enter a name for the template and choose a save location, then click Save.

To use this template to create a new file, all you'll need to do is choose File > New From Template (⌘⇧N/Ctrl+Shift+N) and choose the template file from its saved location. A quick check of the Symbols, Graphic Styles, Swatches, and Character/Paragraph Styles panels should confirm that everything saved correctly. Now you can get to work!

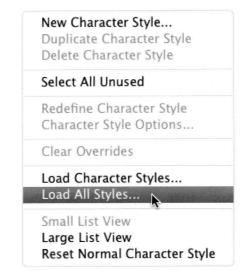

7.57 Select Load All Styles from the Character or Paragraph panel menu…

7.58 …and both sets of styles will be loaded into their respective panels.

Getting Your Work Out of Illustrator

Once you've created a set of screens and/or graphic assets, you'll need to get them out of Illustrator. You might need to show your screens to a client during a meeting, send a PDF to a stakeholder for approval, or slice some images for your dev team. With Illustrator, there are a lot of options for sharing your work, and you have a lot of flexibility in how you can accomplish the task.

Presentation Mode

In my old Photoshop workflow, I would create different screens and states of interaction on various layers, all of which I would have to show or hide as I presented. This meant I had to spend so much time naming and organizing layers so that I knew where everything was. It was a fairly clumsy experience for both the client and me. As I moved my workflow to Illustrator, I followed that same pattern at first. One day, a light came on and I discovered the keys to presenting work from Illustrator, a method I dubbed Presentation mode.

Presentation mode consists of two key elements to work properly:

- Creating screens and interaction states on separate artboards instead of separate layers

- Making full use of Full Screen mode

To see how this works, open the **add-car.ai** file you worked on earlier in the chapter. This file has four screens in sequence to preview an interaction.

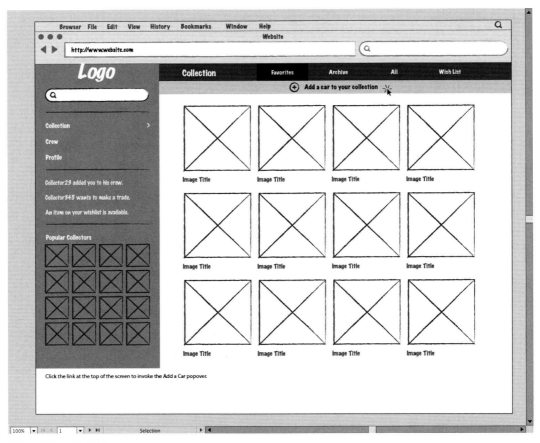

7.59 Presentation mode

Once you have the file open, all you'll need to do is select Full Screen mode from the Change Screen Modes button ⬓ at the bottom of the Tools panel. The window will stretch to fill the screen, all panels will be hidden, and you'll be left with the artboard navigator and scroll bars (**7.59**). Once in this mode, you can use the next and previous buttons in the artboard navigator to step through your screens in sequence.

NOTE If you started reading here, you can download the finished file by going to www.peachpit.com/UIwithAI/ch7/add-car-final.ai.ai.

NOTE If you have a large display, the artboards will fill the screen as you step through them. While this is annoying, you can quickly press ⌘1/Ctrl+1 to zoom to 100%. This doesn't usually happen when displaying your work on a projector, as projector resolutions tend to be lower than desktop displays.

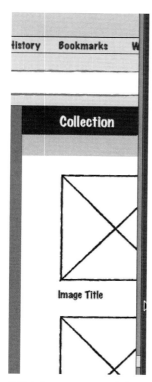

7.60 In Presentation mode, bump your mouse to the edge of the screen…

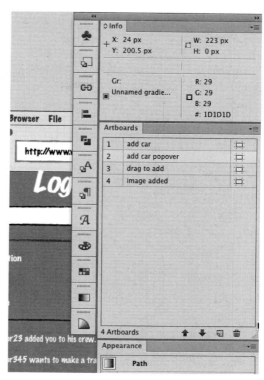

7.61 …to temporarily expand the panels.

If you need to access any of the panels while in Presentation mode, you can drag your mouse to the edge of the screen (**7.60**) and they will slide into view (**7.61**). Move your mouse away from the edge and they will slide back out. If you need to show them for an extended period of time, press Tab to toggle panel visibility.

Exporting to Other Formats

Another way to get your artwork out of Illustrator is to export (File > Export) to one of the various supported file formats. You can export a single artboard, a specified range, or all at once. Illustrator exports to several formats, but the ones most useful for UI design are as follows:

- **PNG:** PNGs are great for images that have large areas of flat color. They are a good alternative to the older GIF format. PNGs support 8-bit transparency like a GIF, but also offer 24-bit alpha transparency for smooth gradations in transparent areas. PNG employs lossless compression, meaning that it can compress your file without losing any data. PNG files support only the RGB color space, so don't use this format if you need to export any CMYK images.

- **Flash:** The Flash exporter allows you to create animations in the Flash SWF format. This can be a great tool for visualizing interactions and previewing how CSS animations might work in the browser.

- **JPEG:** JPEGs are best for photographic images. JPEG offers lossy compression, meaning it discards file data to create the smallest possible file size. This can create artifacts in your images. The more compression you choose, the more artifacts you get.

- **Photoshop:** The Photoshop exporter allows you to save your Illustrator files to Photoshop with layers and editable text. This works well if you need to shuttle graphics back and forth without losing editing flexibility.

TIP When exporting multiple artboards, Illustrator uses the filename plus the artboard name for the name of the exported file. If you don't want to end up with names like "untitled08-01.jpg," be sure to save your Illustrator file first and then give all your artboards meaningful names.

Saving PDFs

If you need to save your Illustrator artboards in a cross platform-compatible vector format, look no further than the Portable Document Format (PDF). PDFs can be viewed by just about anybody, and they don't suffer from any loss of quality like a bitmap file would. Additionally, you can save multiple artboards to a single PDF file, which makes sharing large projects super easy. After presentation mode, PDFs are the best way I have found to share screens with clients for the purpose of reviewing work.

To save an Illustrator file as a PDF, perform the following steps:

1. Create a new file (⌘N/Ctrl+N) with 10 artboards.

2. Choose File > Save As (⌘⇧S/Ctrl+Shift+S). Choose PDF from the Format pop-up at the bottom of the dialog box.

   Under the Format pop-up, there is an option to save all artboards or save a range. Selecting the All radio button will do just as it says, while clicking Range will allow you to specify any number of artboards to save (**7.62**).

   Here are some examples:

   - Entering *1* will save only artboard number 1 as a PDF.

   - Entering *1–4* will save artboards 1 through 4.

   - Entering *1, 3–5, 7, 9–10* will save all but artboards 2, 6, and 8.

7.62 Choosing the PDF format and range of artboards to save

3. Clicking Save will move to the next step in the process, which allows you to specify PDF options.

   The majority of these options are for documents destined for printing, so there is a lot that you won't use in this dialog box.

4. If you're saving this file for sending to a client, you can clear all the checkboxes under the Options section (**7.63**). Otherwise, you can leave each of these options at the default. Click Save PDF to complete the process.

Save for Web

Finally, you can save individual graphics in your Illustrator file as separate files with the Save for Web command (⌘⇧⌥S/ Ctrl+Shift+Alt+S). In order to do this, you'll need to first create the boundaries for each exported file with the Slice tool ✐ (Shift-K). This tool creates slices that are recognized by the Save for Web command as a separate image and will save each slice to its own file. Each slice can have its own format and compression properties.

To learn how to use this command, go to www.peachpit.com/UIwithAI/ch7/slices.ai to download and open the example file. Once you have the file open in Illustrator, do one of the following:

- Select the Slice tool in the Tools panel and drag a box around one of the icons. You can zoom in for more precision if necessary (**7.64**).

  This method allows you to create a precise slice that is independent of the artwork. The slice can be selected, moved, and deleted without affecting the underlying art.

Options
☐ Preserve Illustrator Editing Capabilities
☐ Embed Page Thumbnails
☐ Optimize for Fast Web View
☐ View PDF after Saving
☐ Create Acrobat Layers from Top-Level Layers

7.63 Clear all Options checkboxes for a smaller PDF file.

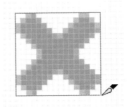

7.64 Creating a slice with the Slice tool

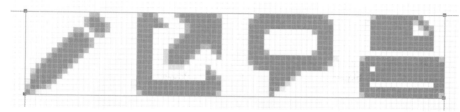

7.65 Creating a slice from a selection

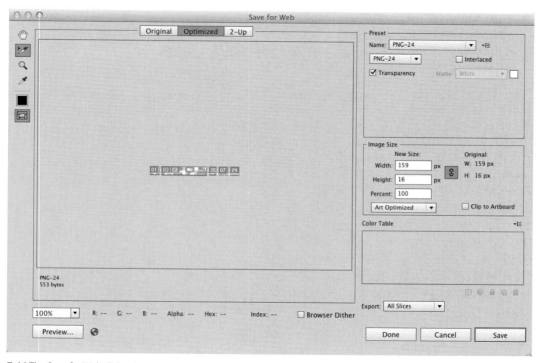

7.66 The Save for Web dialog box

- Select one or more icons and choose Object > Slice > Create from Selection.

  This method creates a slice around the boundaries of your selection (**7.65**).

- Select one or more icons and choose Object > Slice > Make.

  This method creates *user slices*, which are tied to the underlying artwork. If the

artwork dimensions change, the slice automatically adjusts to fit. To remove a user slice, select the object and choose Object > Slice > Release.

Once you have your slices created, choose File > Save for Web. A large dialog box appears with your sliced artwork in the middle (**7.66**). Each slice is designated by a number.

Before you click Save, do the following:

1. Choose the Slice Select tool 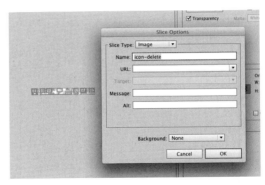 (K) and double-click each slice to give it a name (**7.67**).

   The name you enter in the dialog box will be the name of the exported artwork. If you don't name your slices, Illustrator will name them for you. That's not necessarily a good thing.

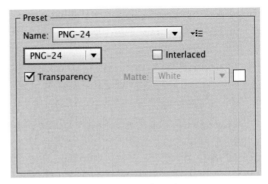

7.67 Naming slices for export

2. Click each icon in turn and choose an export format in the Preset section (**7.68**).

   Each slice can have its own individual settings for complete optimization.

3. Select which slices to export from the Export menu (**7.69**).

   Choosing All Slices will export everything, including slices that Illustrator automatically creates between your artwork. Choosing User Slices will export only slices you created with Object > Slices > Make. Choosing Selected Slices will export only slices you explicitly have selected in the Save for Web dialog box.

4. Click Done to save your settings and return without exporting anything, or click Save to export your selections.

   If you click Done, your Save for Web setting will be saved with the file, allowing you to come back any time and export your artwork.

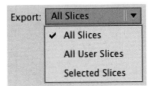

7.68 Choosing an export format for a slice

7.69 Choosing which slices to export

Conclusion

In this book, you've learned which tools work best for UI design; explored color, typography, and layout; and created a sample user interface using graphic styles and symbols. You've also learned how to use Illustrator to help you plan, communicate your efforts, and share your work effectively. With these tools, you're ready to start tackling UI design at a higher level.

I hope I've helped you to see that Illustrator can be a viable tool for UI design, and that you find ways to build on this knowledge and become an Illustrator expert yourself. One last tip: spend some quality time playing with all the tools and features of Illustrator. As you explore the interface, you'll find new ways to use tools and techniques to help you become a power user, going beyond the tips and techniques I've shown you here. Be sure to share what you learn with your friends, coworkers, Twitter followers, and Facebook friends. If you have any comments, feedback, or just want to share, feel free to contact me at rick@rickmoore.me and on Twitter @rmmixd. Keep track of the latest information and updates for the book on Twitter, #UIwithAI.

TABLE 7.1 Keyboard Shortcuts in This Chapter

	MAC	PC
Toggle Smart Guides	⌘U	Ctrl+U
New File	⌘N	Ctrl+N
Save As	⌘⇧S	Ctrl+Shift+S
Save for Web	⌘⇧⌥S	Ctrl+Shift+Alt+S
Unit Preferences	⌘, (comma)	Ctrl+, (comma)

Index

WATCH READ CREATE

Unlimited online access to all Peachpit, Adobe
Press, Apple Training and New Riders videos
and books, as well as content from other
leading publishers including: O'Reilly Media,
Focal Press, Sams, Que, Total Training, John
Wiley & Sons, Course Technology PTR, Class
on Demand, VTC and more.

No time commitment or contract required!
Sign up for one month or a year.
All for $19.99 a month

SIGN UP TODAY
peachpit.com/creativeedge